Carolina Beach Music

from the '60s to the '80s

CAROLINA BEACH MUSIC

from the '60s to the '80s

THE NEW WAVE

Rick Simmons

THE
History
PRESS

Published by The History Press
Charleston, SC 29403
www.historypress.net

Copyright © 2013 by Rick Simmons
All rights reserved

Front: Top left: The Embers; *top right:* Danny Woods of the Chairmen of the Board.
Bottom left: Patti Drew; *bottom right*: The Tower of Power. *Back*: *Top left:* The Spinners;
center: Robert Knight; *bottom right*: William Bell.

First published 2013

Manufactured in the United States

ISBN 978.1.60949.750.7

Library of Congress CIP data applied for.

Contents

Contents

Contents

Acknowledgements, and a Dedication to the Late Billy Scott

When I was working on *Carolina Beach Music: The Classic Years*, I thought that it would be interesting to see if I could interview a few artists to get the inside story about their songs. Roughly half of the one hundred songs I wrote about were accompanied by interviews, and it worked so well that for this book I made interviews a priority. As a result, most of the songs I wrote about in this book benefit from the artists' personal recollections, whether through interviews I did or, if the artists were deceased, by quoting interviews others did with them. In regard to the interviews I conducted, you'd be surprised how hard it is to connect with some of these artists. You would think that anyone with a Web page or Facebook page dedicated to his or her act would be somewhat accessible, and certainly that goes for active performers with agents. Unfortunately, that's not always the case. I have sent dozens of e-mails that have gone unanswered, but if the artist doesn't respond or for some reason doesn't want to be interviewed, so be it—I move on.

But I felt some people simply *had* to be interviewed, and at one point when I was having trouble connecting with some of the artists I remembered that Billy Scott, who I had interviewed twice and who was truly "Mr. Beach Music," had once said he'd help me if I ever needed information about any of the artists—so I took him up on it. I gave him the names of several people I wanted to interview, and he promised to help; within a few days, I had interviewed Jeff Reid, Donny Trexler, Janice Barnett and Roy C. Hammond. Later, when I needed to interview Archie Bell and Jerry Butler to finish the book, Billy arranged that as well. I thanked Billy for his kindness and generosity on a number of occasions, and I also decided that I'd dedicate this book to him for his help. Perhaps my greatest disappointment involving this project was that just after I completed it, Billy passed away in November 2012 and was never able to read here just how much I admired and respected him. In Billy Scott, the beach music industry was fortunate to have a truly gracious gentleman as its spokesperson. I can't overstate how important his help was to me in bringing about the completion of this book, and anyone who is a fan of beach music will miss his music, his enthusiasm and his love for the genre that affected us all in so many ways. I feel fortunate that I was able to call him a friend, even if it was for an all-too-brief span of only a few years.

I would also like to thank the interviewees: Gary Barker, Johnny Barker, Janice Barnett, Archie Bell, William Bell, Bill Bradford, Clyde Brown, Jerry Butler, G.C. Cameron, Emilio Castillo, Clifford Curry, Harry Elston, Jim Gilstrap, Cuba Gooding, Jackie Gore, Roy C. Hammond, Keith Huston, Robert Knight, Ken Knox, Nick Marinelli, Rob Parissi, Charles Pope, Jay Proctor, Jeff Reid, Billy Scott, Bobbie Smith, Bobby Tomlinson, John Townsend and Pat Upton. I'd also like to thank those individuals who, while perhaps not performers on the songs, did help me get the interviews or pictures, offered insight or helped with research: Todd Baptista, Juanita Bell, Charlie Brown, Nat Burgess, Marion Carter, Larry Eaglin, Topher Forhecz, Gerry Gallagher, C. Allen Kotler, Anne Leighton, Rick Levy, Marcia Parks, Chikena Peebles-Crittendon, Dianne Pope, Lorraine Smith, Amanda Tilk and Freddy Tripp. A thanks to my "consultants," Chappy Chapman and Len Hutchison, and especially Steve Bond, my very dear friend who is in the process of winning his fight against cancer. Finally, as always, my love to Sue, Courtenay, Cord, Julie and Dad.

Introduction

After I completed 2011's *Carolina Beach Music: The Classic Years*, I knew that despite the fact that the book examined one hundred pre-1975 beach music classics there were still many more songs that I hadn't covered. This was especially true of the crucial transitional years in beach music history, the late 1970s and early 1980s. So as I turned to my next project, I knew that I not only needed to address the stories behind some of the classic tunes I had left unexplored the first time, but that I also needed to cover some of the newer, transitional, original Carolina beach music.

Since it is unlikely that you are reading this book if you know nothing about beach music, and because I defined it in my last book, I won't attempt to explain what beach music is—as if anyone really can. Suffice it to say that by the mid-'60s, it was an amalgam of R&B music from the '40s, '50s and '60s; recordings by groups that were originally cover bands primarily from the Carolinas; and just about anything that people could "shag" to. The shag was the dance people had been doing to beach music along the coast for decades, and by the 1970s, beach music started to diversify even more. Though it was still primarily soul and rhythm and blues, more upbeat dance music started to work its way onto beach playlists with the rise of disco across the nation. Songs and groups that would primarily be identified with the disco movement produced shaggable music that could fittingly be considered beach music, but the fact that it was disco meant that the music took the beach music sound in a whole new direction. In addition, many well-established and enormously successful national groups that had been considered solid soul/R&B/beach music acts expanded their repertoires in order to keep up with music's new directions and keep their music relevant. This led to a very different sound for some of these groups, but it also meant that many of the songs they recorded were accepted much more quickly as part of the beach music canon than would have otherwise been the case.

But perhaps the most dynamic change, and what truly changed beach music forever, was that groups both local and national started to produce self-aware beach music beginning in the mid- to late 1970s. This principally started after the Catalinas' 1975 recording "Summertime's Calling Me" became a huge regional favorite. Here was a song written about the beach, by a group from the Carolinas, and the group apparently had nothing more ambitious in mind than having the song be a hit on the beach music circuit. It eventually became just that, and after the song's regional success, groups that had recorded classic-era hits but that principally played the beach music circuit by this point also started to record songs about the beach geared for a beach music audience. These well-established acts lent credibility to regional beach music that might otherwise have been slow to gain acceptance. This was especially true of the contributions of the Chairmen of the Board, who had not only had a number of Top 40 hits in the early '70s but who also led the charge with some of the greatest original compositions of the new age of beach music. As Jeff Reid, writer of "Myrtle Beach Days" and former member of the Fantastic Shakers, told me, it also benefited the local groups that played the beach circuit with them. "I always thought General Johnson was different from us because he'd had national hits," Reid said. "We'd play with them, like the time in 1980 in Columbia at the stadium, and there'd be six thousand to eight thousand people at a beach concert."

Sharing the stage with more established acts helped the newer acts in the late '70s and early '80s, which were able to break onto the scene without a national recording if the song was good and an original Carolina beach music composition. Groups began to find an audience without having had that big national release, and while it's true that not all of the groups with classic-era hits had had national releases, it certainly wasn't for lack of trying. But in many ways, by the late '70s, a recording contract with a national label, no matter how briefly it ran, was no longer a prerequisite for being taken seriously as a beach music act.

It was inevitable that this had to happen. As General Johnson later wrote of his founding of Surfside Records with Mike Branch in 1979, "Our objective was to record new music to revitalize the identity of a thriving [beach] music market that was slowly being recognized as too dependent on old recordings." Certainly it's true that just a few hundred classic-era beach music hits couldn't carry the industry forever. As acts and individuals grew older and passed on, it would mean that every beach music song performed live would be a cover version, and that certainly would have relegated beach music to an amateurishness that the genre perhaps could not have survived. And while some of the newer beach songs may have sounded like amateur efforts, audiences started to adopt those songs as their own primarily because they were tired of the same old classic-era hits. Unexpectedly, beginning in the 1980s this led to a disturbing trend by some groups to re-record updated versions of those classics, prompting one classic-era artist I interviewed to tell me, "I hear so many repos and sound-alikes it makes me sick." For the most part, I agree—I'm generally not interested in hearing new recordings of the songs covered in this book or the last. But to each his own.

As a result, there were enough classic tunes from the late '60s that I didn't cover the first time, national-level songs from the '70s that qualified as good beach music and seminal tunes from the period that marked the rise of original Carolina beach music that I felt this book had to examine songs from all three categories. In order to cover a few classics I missed last time, bridge a few gaps and address the rise of original Carolina beach music, the focus this time is on the years 1966 to 1982. I also revisited a few songs I wrote about last time as a result of interviews that shed new light on those previously covered songs.

This book, then, covers some of those classic beach music tunes as well as the newer self-aware songs that were the beginning of a new wave of beach music that has turned into something altogether different today. We hear the last vestiges of the Funk Brothers–driven Motown sound, Memphis soul and classic R&B sound giving way to the sounds of Philadelphia, the rise of disco and finally a movement by regional beach bands that seemed satisfied if their music was only popular in the Carolinas. This became the beach sound that would eventually lead the music to where it is today, inspire a redefinition of beach music and bridge the gap between the classic era and the Carolina beach music that would eventually emerge as a formidable force in its own right.

A final note: because last time I cut down interviews and entries to make a suitable word count for the publisher, I determined that this time I'd try and do fewer songs (eighty as opposed to one hundred) and cover them a bit more thoroughly. In most cases this means I was able to provide more details about the songs, which I think makes hearing them after knowing the stories behind them all that much better. I'd encourage you to crank up your jukebox, stereo or iPod as you read along, and listen for those musical moments the artists told me about. Hear for yourself why Jerry Butler told me the greatness of "Western Union Man" is due to "the way Leon Huff plays piano" and why Harry Elston of the Friends of Distinction said that Charlene Gibson "flat out tore it up" singing lead on "Love or Let Me Be Lonely"; listen closely and hear Melba Moore, Nick Ashford and Valerie Simpson's backing vocals on "Apples, Peaches, Pumpkin Pie," how Clyde Brown and Johnny Moore trade the lead on the Drifters' "More than a Number" and how the "steady step" that Robert Knight explains he added to "Everlasting Love" made it a hit. Unfortunately, by covering fewer songs this time, that means there are still a lot of significant songs I haven't yet written about; perhaps I'll get to those in the future.

Barbara Acklin

"Love Makes a Woman"
1968, Billboard #15
Brunswick 55379

"Am I the Same Girl"
1969, Billboard #79
Brunswick 55399

If she had done nothing but *write* songs, the late Barbara Acklin would have left an indelible mark on R&B and beach music. However, the multi-talented Acklin was a singer and a songwriter, and while perhaps not a household name today, her performances on "Love Makes a Woman" and "Am I the Same Girl" have ensured that, for beach music lovers, her contributions to the genre will not be forgotten.

Barbara Acklin moved to Chicago when she was five, and after high school, like several other aspiring female soul singers during the 1960s (most notably Diana Ross and Martha Reeves), she first worked as a secretary at a record company while waiting for her big break. In this case the record company was St. Lawrence Records, and under the name Barbara Allen she recorded a song on the Special Agent label, though it failed to chart. Acklin also did backup work for Chicago singers such as Etta James and Fontella Bass, and by 1966, she had moved to Brunswick Records to work as a receptionist while trying to land a contract as a solo act.

That first big break did come, though it had nothing to do with her singing. Along with her friend David Scott, she co-wrote a song called "Whispers" and took it to Brunswick's biggest act, Jackie Wilson, who at the time hadn't had a Top 20 hit since 1963. Wilson liked the song and recorded it, and by the fall of 1966, "Whispers" hit #11 on the pop charts and his music was relevant once again (he'd follow up with "Higher and Higher"

and "I Get the Sweetest Feeling"—beach music classics all). As Acklin told Bob Pruter, Wilson said, "If there is anything I can do for you, let me know." Acklin told him to tell the record company she wanted to cut a record of her own, and Wilson was true to his word. "About three weeks later, I was in the studio," she said.

Her first solo efforts didn't do much, but Brunswick label mate Gene Chandler had heard her sing and decided it might be a good idea to record a couple duets with her. While the first, "Show Me the Way to Go," did okay, going to #30 on the R&B charts, the second, "From the Teacher to the Preacher," went to #57 on the pop charts and #16 on the R&B charts. But it was her solo hit, the beach standard "Love Makes a Woman," that really helped Acklin make a name for herself. It had that pop/R&B crossover feel that a number of female soul artists such as Patti Drew, Millie Jackson and Freda Payne would find success with in the late '60s and early '70s, and the song went to #15 on the pop charts and #3 on the R&B charts and would win a BMI award.

At this point, Acklin had the pedigree to be taken seriously as a major up-and-comer, but oddly enough, it was her own record company that hindered her success. Acklin had recorded a song called "Am I the Same Girl" backed by the instrumental stylings of the Brunswick studio musicians, and listening to it today, it's obvious it should have been a hit. Apparently, though, the record company liked the instrumental portion better than the vocals; they removed Acklin's vocal track and added another piano section instead. They re-titled the song "Soulful Strut" and released it as being by Young-Holt Unlimited (though neither Young nor Holt actually played on the track!), and in 1968, it went to #3 in the United States and #1 in Canada. It sold two million copies—and Acklin was livid. She told Pruter, "I had originally recorded [it], and they took my voice off and added a piano…I was pretty ticked off about that, but you know, that's what happens." Brunswick finally released her version in 1969 with the vocals, but by that time, it probably sounded like she was copying Young-Holt instead of the other way around. Her version stalled at #79, though it was popular in the Carolinas.

Acklin would have a few more chart hits, but she would never make a substantial mark as a singer. She would continue to write songs though and would co-write several of the Chi-Lites' hits, the biggest being "Have You Seen Her," which was #3 on the pop charts and #1 on the R&B charts. Her own solo career would eventually wind down, and she would go on to sing backup for acts such as the Chi-Lites and Tyrone Davis before passing away in 1998.

The Band of Oz

"Shaggin'"
1978, did not chart
Mega 18830

"Ocean Boulevard"
1982, did not chart
Surfside 820310

Billy Bazemore was our lead vocalist, and he came in one day and said, 'Look, I gotta set of lyrics here, I've written a song,'" Band of Oz founder Keith Houston told the author. "Well, he pulls out *four pages* of lyrics—it was probably three or four songs! I took it and edited down and put the music to it. And though we had two or three songs worth of lyrics, we did get one real good hit out of it." That hit song was "Shaggin'," the band's first recording and one of several beach music hits released regionally in 1978 that were largely responsible for bridging the gap between the era of national releases adopted by shaggers in the Carolinas and the new era of beach music when music was being written specifically for them.

The Band of Oz started in Grifton, North Carolina, in the late 1960s as the Avengers, and the core of the group consisted of Johnnie Byrd, Buddy Johnson and Keith Houston. By 1970, they had changed their name to the Band of Oz, and the addition of horns saw them expand their lineup as they played part time at fraternity parties and on the club circuit. By the mid-'70s,

The Band of Oz. *Courtesy of Keith Houston.*

they had become a full-time band, and members Chuck French, Bob Lynch, Ronnie Forbes, Shep Fields, Freddy Tripp, Billy Bazemore, David Hicks and Keith Houston played a daunting schedule throughout the South. "We'd been playing full time traveling all over the Southeast," Houston said, "but we were all tired of being on the road. We figured that since back in the late '60s and early '70s we had played a lot of beach music—even though it wasn't called that then—we could go back to North Carolina and do that type of music again. The disco era was fading, and so we came back home, started playing the old beach music that we used to play. It was actually getting big then, and new beach music was being written as well."

The band decided to try their hand at the new music too. "'Shaggin'' was written in 1978, and it came out at about the same time as 'I Love Beach Music' by the Embers and 'Myrtle Beach Days' by the Shakers," he said. After Bazemore gave his group the lyrics and Houston whittled them down into one good song, they tested it out by playing it in their act. "We actually put it together and were playing it live before we ever made the record. We felt very positive about it based on that and decided to record it. It was the first time our band had actually been in the studio." The band went to Mega Sound in Bailey, North Carolina, and recorded the song with Bazemore singing lead. "You never know what's going to happen when you make a record," Houston said, "but we got a good response. We started pushing it at the radio stations. All the beach jocks started to play it, and it got a lot of airplay. Then when Ripete Records came in and put together that first Beach Beat album, and it had 'Shaggin'' on it along with 'Myrtle Beach Days,' 'I Love Beach Music' and a lot of national releases, it locked it in as a beach music hit."

At first, nothing they did could really follow up "Shaggin'" as far as audiences were concerned, and even though "we recorded another song about that time, 'Song of My Life,' it never did anything, because 'Shaggin'' overshadowed it." There were a few more personnel changes, and in 1982, another big hit came along—actually, one that was even bigger—when they recorded "Ocean Boulevard," which was written and produced by General Johnson and Warren Moise. "Warren wrote it, and he came in when we were working with the General and said he had a song for us. The General wanted us to do it, but the lyrics were horrendous," Houston told me. "We said we didn't want to record it. The General said, 'No, you're going to cut it, and this is what we're going to do. We'll redo the lyrics tonight, and you'll have good lyrics for it tomorrow.' So we went in and cut the music the first day, we left the studio with the tracks down. That night, he and Warren went in and completely rewrote the lyrics, and when we did the vocals the next day, it was like a completely different song." Though it may be hard to believe today that the song that went on to win song of the year at the Carolina Beach Music Awards initially had "lyrics so bad we weren't going to do it," Houston insists that was the case. "Warren wrote a lot of great songs, but that one was a mess at first."

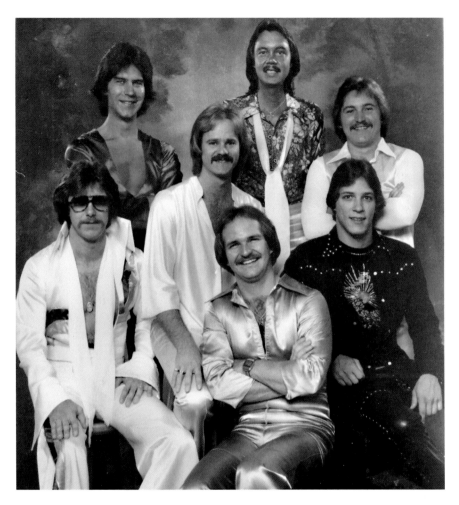

The Band of Oz. *Courtesy of Keith Houston.*

The awards and accolades have followed the Band of Oz almost nonstop over the years, as have songs that they have come to be known for as their repertoire has expanded. In fact, Houston says there have been so many that "we don't play 'Shaggin'" all that much now. Even though it was one of the biggest selling things we did, we only play it once in a great while. We get more requests for 'Shama Lama Ding Dong' and 'Over the Rainbow' than 'Shaggin'' and 'Ocean Boulevard.' But you know, I think it's one of those things that if we did it every night, we'd be indoctrinating another group of kids, because most people are more familiar with the newer stuff. But they are still great songs." And even though they might not play those older hits as much as they used to, they still stand as seminal beach music songs that came out as the genre was making its transition from a collection of national releases appropriated for use as beach music to a genre that was increasingly creating songs all its own.

Archie Bell and the Drells

"TIGHTEN UP"
1968, Billboard #1
Atlantic 2478

"I CAN'T STOP DANCING"
1968, Billboard #9
Atlantic 2534

"THERE'S GONNA BE A SHOWDOWN"
1968, Billboard #21
Atlantic 2583

"GIRL YOU'RE TOO YOUNG"
1969, Billboard #59
Atlantic 2644

"MY BALLOON'S GOING UP"
1969, Billboard #87
Atlantic 2663

"DANCING TO YOUR MUSIC"
1973, Billboard #61
Glades 1707

"I COULD DANCE ALL NIGHT"
1975, did not chart
TSOP 4767

I've always been a guy who wanted to do music to uplift people," Archie Bell told me. "I want my music to make them get up and move." If there's one certainty about Archie Bell and the Drells and their music, it's that it will definitely make you want to get up and move. Perhaps that's why few groups have as many solid beach music classic hits as Archie Bell and the Drells.

Native Texan Archie Bell first formed his group with some friends in 1966. "We started out as just the Drells," he told me. "L.C. Watts, who left the group before we became famous, loved the Dells and added the 'r' to come up with 'Drells.' We always said that a Drell is an excellent entertainer and a perfect gentleman. It was only later when I came to be seen as the frontman that we went to Archie Bell and the Drells, and my name just happened to rhyme." They recorded some sides for the Ovide label, including "Tighten Up," but at about that time Bell was drafted and his music career, it seemed, was on hold—if not over.

As Bell was getting used to army life, the record was selling by the truckload in Texas, despite the fact that the group's manager, disc jockey Skipper Lee Frazier, had been pushing the flipside, "Dog Eat Dog," as the A-side. Once "Tighten Up" was promoted as the hit, with its leadoff that proudly proclaimed they were "Archie Bell and the Drells from Houston, Texas," sales took off in the South. "I said that about being from Texas because after the Kennedy assassination I heard a DJ say nothing good had ever come out of Texas," Bell told me. "I knew that wasn't true, and that was my way of making a statement." It certainly didn't hurt sales, as the record sold several hundred thousand copies regionally before coming to the attention of Atlantic Records, which released it nationally and watched it sell one million records, climb all the way to #1 and earn a gold record in 1968. Everyone was shocked, and no one more so than Bell. "We never thought 'Tighten Up' would be as big as it was," he said. "It was a real surprise to everybody." Perhaps even more so because other than Bell's lead, there was almost no participation by the rest of the group on the record. The backbone of the song is the instrumental work of a Texas group, the TSU Tornadoes, and save some hand clapping and whistling, the Drells don't contribute much else.

But stranger still, Bell told the author he had to both hear about and enjoy the record's success from a hospital bed in Germany. "After I was drafted, I served in the Fifty-third Transportation Unit stationed in Germany. I'd been in a wreck and was in the hospital when my manager called me and told me that 'Tighten Up' has just gone gold. Earlier I'd been telling the guys I served with, 'Hey, that music you hear on the radio, that's me.' One of them said, 'You guys from Texas sure can tell some big lies! I guess that's because everything's big in Texas!' They didn't believe me. But when Skipper called me, I rolled my wheelchair down the hall and told my buddies my record had gone gold, and they realized what I'd been telling them was really true—it really WAS me! Suddenly I had an entourage! We'd be on bivouac, and there'd be twelve men trying to get in a four-man tent! Everywhere I went, people knew me. There was a paper called the *Overseas Weekly*, and about two weeks later, they had an article there about me that said I was 'the richest GI in the army since Elvis!' It was really all a dream."

But it could have been a nightmare. The group needed to follow up their big hit, but that was pretty hard to do while their frontman was stationed in Germany. Fortunately, the army was pretty liberal with Bell after "Tighten Up" became a hit and frequently allowed him to go home for a few days to perform. One of those trips resulted in a meeting that was to pay big dividends. "After 'Tighten Up' came out, we were in Longside, New Jersey, in a bar called Loretta's High Hat. The manager had connections with the Philadelphia music scene, and after the show, Kenny Gamble and Leon Huff came into the dressing room, though I didn't know who they were. They said they liked 'Tighten Up' and told me, 'We've got a song for you.'" Atlantic was excited that Gamble and Huff wanted to work with the group, and their first collaboration was 1968's "I Can't Stop Dancing." It was a strong follow-up for "Tighten Up," going to #9 on the pop charts, perhaps because it closely followed the same formula as their previous hit. "If you listen to 'Tighten Up' and 'I Can't Stop,' they have almost the same riffs, tempo and everything, except 'Tighten Up' was a jam," Bell told me. "It turned out to be a big, big number for us."

And now the formula was in place. A Gamble and Huff–penned and/or –produced song featuring Bell's smooth vocals meant a hit was almost sure to result. But Gamble and Huff weren't above taking some direction from the boys from Texas either, as was the case with their next hit, "There's Gonna Be a Showdown." "Gamble and Huff were in Houston, and we used to do a sock hop, a big dance party for this radio station," Bell said. "All the people would get together and have those dance competitions, and they'd have this thing called a 'showdown.' They'd form a big circle and put money in a hat, and the one who ended up winning would win the pot. Well, every time you would win, you'd put a notch on your shoe. That's why the words to the song say 'I got ten notches, on my shoes'—that's where that came from. So Gamble and Huff saw us doing it, and they came up with 'Hey man, they tell me you think you're pretty good. But don't you know you're in my neighborhood?'" All of the verses came together to create a finished product that peaked at #21 for their third big hit of 1968. As Bell also noted, while "'Tighten Up' was big here, 'Showdown' was our first big hit in England," where it went to #36. The year 1968 culminated in an album, *Tighten Up*, which hit #15 on the R&B charts and #142 on the pop charts.

In 1969, Bell would finally be mustered out of the army, leaving him free to tour with the group and record more material as the need arose. That year, the group would also release two more songs that would go on to be beach music favorites, "Girl You're Too Young" and "My Balloon's Going Up." "'Girl You're Too Young' was a song I wrote about a young lady I was interested in, but she was little bit too young," Bell said. "That's why it goes 'You're just a baby…,' in the same spirit as 'Go Away Little Girl.'" Bell told me that Elvis gave him some advice about that very subject when he said, "'Archie, fifteen [years old] will get you thirty [years], baby!' I said, 'Yeah, Elvis, but you married a fourteen-year-old!' 'Yeah,' he said, 'but I got her parents' permission!'" "Girl You're Too Young" would peak at #59 on the pop charts and #13 on the R&B charts, and their very next release would be another classic, "My Balloon's Going Up." "That was another Gamble and Huff number, and that was the type of song that could have been in a Broadway play or movie," he said. "It's about a guy who's losing his girlfriend. The balloon was his love, going up, getting away from her. He's saying, 'I'll find a new love.'" Though it peaked at #87, Bell says it was big with beach music audiences because "it was danceable, and it's the type of song you can shag to easily. What we called the old soft shoe."

"Balloon" was their last high-charter on Atlantic, and after seven more Atlantic singles, none of which made the Top 40, they left the label in 1972. The fledgling Miami-based Glades label, however, was all too happy to sign a group of the Drells' caliber and pedigree. "They had come to us and said, 'Come on, Archie, record with us—we have a smash for you.' Everybody's got a smash, you know," Bell said. They did sign with Glades, but they were soon in for a shock after working with a long-established label like Atlantic. "When we signed with the label and went down there, they were supposed to have all this music prepared for us, ready to record. But when I arrived, I had to sit down with Steve Alaimo and KC [later to find fame with the Sunshine Band] and write the words with them. I told my manager, 'I thought this stuff was supposed to be ready? This is not going to work.'" But he admits that their biggest song for the label, "Dancing to Your Music," was a great record. "We recorded it down in Muscle Shoals, Alabama. They wanted us to keep that 'Tighten Up' pattern with a dance song, and it was a great song, one of my favorites. 'Never had the nerve

before to get up on the floor, I'm spinning round and round, really getting down, got me screaming for more. I'm dancing to your music.' You know what he means, whatever the girl says goes—he's dancing to her music. I really liked that song." But despite Bell's enthusiasm about "Dancing to Your Music," it only went to #61 on the pop charts and #11 on the R&B charts and would in fact be their last entry ever on the pop charts. And they were also done with Glades. "We made the one trip down there and never went back. We were with the label for about a year. They didn't pay their royalties either, and they ripped a lot of people off," he says.

"After it didn't work out with Glades, I called Gamble and Huff and told them we'd like to sign with their label," Bell said, "and they were real receptive." They signed with the TSOP subsidiary of Philadelphia International, a '70s soul label with acts such as the O'Jays and Harold Melvin and the Blue Notes. They were given another song in the dance-mode genre, 1975's "I Could Dance All Night." "It was the disco era by then," Bell said, "and we used to work in New York at Studio 54 and places like that. The show would kick off at 10:00 p.m., and when you'd come out of the club, it would be daylight—and you'd have been dancing all night! In the disco era, that's exactly what happened." Though the song didn't make the pop charts, it did rise to #25 on the R&B charts and was a good start for their time at TSOP.

Over the next four years, they had R&B chart hits twice more on TSOP and then four times on Philadelphia International. But as time went on, they didn't feel they were getting quite the attention some of the other groups were getting, and this and other factors led to them finally deciding to call it quits in 1979. Bell went solo for a while, but despite an album and a few singles, solo success was elusive. Today Bell still tours, cranking out those great tunes for fans across the nation.

In retrospect, from the late '60s to the mid-'70s, Archie Bell and the Drells produced some of the best dance tunes ever recorded. Because, in a sense, dancing is the essence of beach music, it has made for a perfect marriage between their music and the beach music community.

William Bell

"Easy Comin' Out (Hard Goin' In)"
1977, did not chart
Mercury 73961

"Easy Comin' Out (Hard Goin' In)' may sound like it's a double-entendre, but it's actually a clean song," William Bell told the author. "It's written about how it's easy to get out of the house but hard getting back in when you've been out all night. But it wasn't intentionally written to sound like a double-entendre—it just worked out that way." The song with the salacious-sounding title is actually just one of many R&B hits by Bell, but it's this soulful tune above all of his others that is considered a beach music classic.

William Bell recorded first as a member of the Del Rios in the late 1950s, but in 1961 he recorded his first solo effort for Stax, a song he had written called "You Don't Miss Your Water." Though the song would only reach #95 on the Billboard Hot 100, it was the beginning of a long, productive relationship with Stax that would see Bell regarded as one of its top draws. Though his career was interrupted by a stint in the army from 1962 to 1966, he recorded enough material while on leave that Stax was able to continue releasing his material even though he was no longer a civilian. After his enlistment was up, Bell had another Top 100 hit with "Everybody Loves a Winner" in 1967, and over the next two years, many of his releases would perform fairly well on the pop charts and the R&B charts. As his songwriting talents evolved, he would also write and co-write hits for other artists, most notably for Albert King ("Born Under a Bad Sign," which would also be covered by Cream) and "I Forgot to Be Your Lover," which Bell recorded in 1968 and which would be recorded by Billy Idol as "To Be a Lover" and go to the #6 position on the pop charts in 1986.

Perhaps the most notable recording to come out of his Stax years was 1968's "Private Number," a duet with Judy Clay (see that entry later in this book). But even in the midst of so much personal songwriting and performing success, Bell saw that Stax was in trouble. After its biggest star, Otis Redding, died in 1967, the label lost its distribution deal with Atlantic Records in 1968 and started to overextend itself and make some poor financial decisions. "The downfall of Stax was kind of systematic deflation of the label by the powers that be," Bell told me. "There was money borrowed, and when you say you'll release fifty thousand records for a new William Bell single, and then once you get into that borrowed money you only release five thousand records instead, automatically your earning potential has diminished. A lot of people don't realize it, but we had two or three hit records on the charts when Stax folded. But the thing about it was that we weren't selling as many records. [The public] loved the artists and loved the production and everything, but we weren't competitive in the market. We were forced out of the business because we had to make monthly payments on these huge loans, and with the diminishing numbers of pressed products, if it wasn't pressed, we couldn't sell it, so we were forced to file bankruptcy."

"I'd gone to Stax as a young kid and never thought that would end," Bell says. "But at that point, I decided I wasn't going to record anymore and I was going to do something else." But he was soon contacted by his old friend Charles Fach, who was now with Mercury. "Mercury wasn't known for a lot of R&B products, but Charlie had his finger on the pulse of R&B and he talked me into going back into recording." As a result, Bell agreed to give recording another try, but on one condition: "One of the contractual stipulations I set up was that as long as Charlie was with Mercury, I'd remain." That clause was to be significant within a very short time.

Bell's first release for his new label, a song he'd co-written, was to be the biggest of his career. "Trying to Love Two" was a big hit, peaking at #10 on the pop charts and #1 on the R&B charts. He followed this with another song, "Coming Back for More," that, while not a huge hit, did at least make the R&B charts. Up next was what would be his third—and, as it turned out, final—release for Mercury, "Easy Comin' Out (Hard Goin' In)." "After the two previous singles, Mercury was pressing me for a new

William Bell. *Courtesy of William Bell.*

record, and I sat down over a period of about three months and wrote a lot of songs, and this was the first of those. The song was written during the disco period, which was kind of a wild period. It was kind of adopted at Studio 54 in New York and just really turned out to be a double-entendre-type thing. It was written just as a clean-minded, clean-cut song, but it turned out to be a good record for us." The song peaked at #30 on the R&B charts, the third Mercury single in a row to chart.

Bell thinks "Easy Comin' Out" would have done even better, however, but changes occurring at Mercury at the time hurt the record's promotion. "Right about that time, there was some corporate upheaval at Mercury and Charles left. When I found out, I realized that with Charles gone there was nobody there who really knew what I was about, and I knew then the writing was on the wall, so I set up a meeting with them." Bell told them that per the stipulation in his contract, he would be leaving, and after that it was obvious to him that Mercury quit pushing "Easy Comin' Out," even as it was moving up the charts. "It probably could have been bigger, and I was disappointed by 'Easy's' performance—it never got promoted the way 'Tryin to Love Two' did. With the upheaval going on at Mercury, it was clear that there wasn't all that cohesive a promotional staff, and so nobody was really working on that aspect of the record. Then, after I asked for my release, within about three weeks the record dropped completely off the charts. That shows you what was going on in the collective effort from a corporate standpoint there." Bell wasn't naive, however, and knew why the record disappeared from the charts. "I understood their position though. They knew I wasn't going to stay on as one of their artists, so why should they promote the record?" If he needed further proof of the label's disinterest in his music at that point, Mercury did hold him to a contractual agreement that said he owed them one more album—which he recorded but which was never released. In any event, Bell was done with Mercury: "I got my release after delivering the album."

Bell would continue to record, and his songs would continue to chart right up until the mid-1990s. He is still a popular performer today, and though his shows feature a number of his chart hits, "Easy Comin' Out" "is one of my biggest songs now. It's one of the staple songs in my repertoire. I can't leave the stage without performing it, and if I don't perform it, I'm in trouble. It's very popular." Bell says that this supports his belief that if Mercury had done a better job promoting the record, it probably would have been bigger than it was.

Bell was honored to be inducted into the Beach Music Hall of Fame in 2004. "It feels great to be in the Beach Music Hall of Fame," he said. "It actually validates your body of work. Even though a lot of the songs are R&B, it feels really good to have that different audience, and I was just tickled to death when I found out I would be inducted. I think the beach music audience is one of the best audiences in the world as far as its fan base. If you're below the Mason-Dixon line, you know beach music! But it has fans all over the world." Perhaps that's why Bell, who has legions of fans all over the world, is such a good fit for the Beach Music Hall of Fame himself.

Bradford and Bell

"(THEY CALL IT) MR. DOLLAR'S"
1980, did not chart
Spirit 101

J ohnny Dollar's was a very popular beach club in Charlotte in the late '70s," Bill Bradford told me. "One Sunday, Sandy Bell and I were in my apartment, and he was noodling at the keyboard and started singing about going down to Johnny Dollar's because we were going there to get a beer later that afternoon. I said, 'Whoa, you might have something there.' So I ran over and got my handheld cassette recorder and let him play into it, and I said, 'Let's come back to that later on. We might have an idea.'" And have an idea they did; within a year, Bradford and Bell's "(They Call It) Mr. Dollar's" was being played on jukeboxes up and down the coast, making the duet—and the club—very well known throughout the Carolinas.

Bill Bradford noted that when he was a child he loved music, and he'd respond to "anything that had a beat." It was in the third or fourth grade when he caught on to R&B. "I just gravitated towards it," he says. "I don't really have an explanation for that interest, and it astonished my parents. But that somehow was a bit of hardwiring I developed at an early age." Though he played the piano, at that point he wasn't pursuing a musical career, though he did collect records. "I remember listening to records and listening *through* them to try and understand how they did what they did and got the sound they did and how they balanced the instruments and all that. I don't know where that came from, but that was a real interest I had." As he finished college and settled down, "about 1975 I started to think I could write music, so I bought a four-track recorder and set up a little studio in my apartment. It's almost like somebody decides they want to paint and sets up a studio and experiments by themselves. That's what I did for three or four years."

By this time, Bradford had become friends with Sandy Bell, who was a keyboard and blues harp player. They started talking about putting together a record label but knew that "unless we had an idea, or a way to break in, it was going to be tough. We knew that in the Carolinas there were a lot of stations that played beach music, and we decided that that might be our wedge into a market." But they didn't have a song or even much of an idea at that point, until that afternoon when Bell started playing with the makings of a song about going to Charlotte hotspot and beach club Johnny Dollar's.

After recording their initial idea that Sunday, "we went down and had a nice afternoon at the club. In the weeks after that we really thought that it might be a good idea to develop it into a song and see if the club owner would allow us to put it on his jukebox." However, they were limited by the equipment they had, primarily because "we were both working other jobs and didn't have the time or the money to pay studio musicians and buy time and all the stuff you had to do to make a record." On the flipside, "the equipment we had was about what a well-equipped Atlantic Records studio might have had about 1955. Since a lot of the classic beach music had that sound—the Clovers, Coasters, Drifters—we decided to give it a try. We said, 'Let's try to produce the best classic '50s R&B sound that we can, because we've got the means to do that, and have this song sound like something you might have heard in 1959 or 1960.' So the sound of the tune was intentional in that way." With Bradford singing lead, they completed the song, pressed some demos and arranged a meeting with Bob Whitman, who owned Johnny Dollar's. They hoped to at least get him to put the record on the club's jukebox, and so one night after the club closed, they played the song for him. "You know, we were scared to death, because this was going to be the make or break. But he loved it, and he said, 'Yeah, I'll put it on my box.'" They had five hundred copies pressed ("which took everything we had in the bank"), took Whitman a copy for his jukebox and at the club the record seemed to play nonstop. It was popular, which "showed we had a good sound and a record that people would respond to, and along with all the other stuff on the jukebox it would be a seamless transition and people would keep dancing—which was important to us." The song's popularity was not without its faults, however. "At one point it played so much the employees were sick of it, and Bob said they had to take it off the box!"

Knowing that they had a good record, Bradford says the next step was to get the record out to more than just the club. "We got the boxes of records and threw them in the back of my car, and Sandy and I both took a week off and went to Myrtle Beach and from there to all of the major cities in South Carolina that had radio stations that played beach music." The record's reception was generally good, and they hit the radio stations, clubs and record stores, leaving copies wherever anyone would play them. Bradford notes that before long, the record was even playing in places they didn't expect. "Two months later, we got a letter from a bar in New York that said we got this record on our jukebox. It just started popping!" Before long, the song was a regional hit, and within a very short time it was even included on beach music compilation albums alongside those classic tunes by the Drifters, the Clovers and other groups whose sounds they had tried to emulate.

As the first release on the Spirit record label, the song was responsible for starting what has become a very successful company today. "Looking back on it, it set Spirit Records in motion. We absolutely had to have a record to get a label going and to make initial contacts and get a way into the musical stream, and 'Johnny Dollar's' was what got it going. It was a blessing in many ways." Bradford says he and Bell still play the song occasionally though neither of them are now full-time members of a band, but he will always be proud of, and thankful for, the record. As for the importance of beach music in the Carolinas, "beach music was endemic to this part of the country and important to the lives of a lot of people. It was about great times and great music—and still is." And "Mr. Dollar's" is and was a part of that legacy as well.

Jerry Butler

"I Dig You Baby"
1966, Billboard #60
Mercury 72648

"Never Give You Up"
1968, Billboard #20
Mercury 72798

"Hey Western Union Man"
1968, Billboard #16
Mercury 72850

"Only the Strong Survive"
1969, Billboard #4
Mercury 72898

"Moody Woman"
1969, Billboard #24
Mercury 72929

"What's the Use of Breaking Up"
1969, Billboard #20
Mercury 72960

"(I'M JUST THINKING ABOUT) COOLING OUT"
1978, did not chart
Philadelphia International 3656

K enny Gamble, Leon Huff and I got together to write a few songs,"
Jerry Butler told the author. "So we went up to this resort up in the
Pennsylvania mountains and sat down and just started talking about just
cooling out, getting away, taking a break from the routine. That's how the
title of 'Cooling Out' came about." And nobody knows cool better than
"the Ice Man" Jerry Butler, who has a very long string of national and beach
music hits to show for it.

Jerry Butler got his start on the Chicago music scene, and he performed
briefly with a few different groups before settling in with the Roosters along
with co-members Curtis Mayfield, Arthur and Richard Brooks and Sam
Gooden. When the group signed with Vee-Jay, their name was changed to
the Impressions, and their first recording was a song Brooks and Butler had
written called "For Your Precious Love." It topped out at #11 in 1958, but
despite the group's success, Butler decided to go solo in 1960. Having been
given the nickname "the Ice Man" for his smooth and cool delivery, Butler
recorded a number of hits for Vee-Jay over the next five years, including "He
Will Break Your Heart" (#7, 1960), "Moon River" (#11, 1962) and "Make It
Easy on Yourself" (#20, 1962). When Vee-Jay went bankrupt, Butler signed
with Mercury for what some might say was the third and most consistently
productive phase of his career.

His second release for Mercury was 1966's "I Dig You Baby," a smooth,
soulful song that, though it would only peak at #60, would also go on to
become a very big song on the Carolina beach music scene. "The interesting
thing about it is that when you said you wanted to ask about some songs,
that's one of the first ones that popped into my mind," Butler told me. "The
original version was done by Lorraine Ellison and produced by Jerry Ross,
and he produced mine too," he said. But I told Butler that I had once heard
he didn't like to sing the song, and he expressed that it was frankly because
the song was somewhat dated. "That happened because of the etymology
of the song," he said. "The expression 'I dig you baby' connotes the hipness
of being. But I was performing it, and a boy said, 'That's so square!' because
the youth had moved beyond that expression. Because of that, I think I was
intimidated, and for a long time I didn't want to sing it anymore!"

While the recording was a good start for him at Mercury, it was when
he was able to start working with Kenny Gamble and Leon Huff that his

records really started to take off. "I met Kenny through Jerry Ross after I recorded 'You Don't Know What You Got,' a Kenny Gamble composition. I told Jerry, 'This guy has a way of putting things, and I think he's very creative and unique.' Later, I was in Philadelphia and I met Gamble and Huff and I was complimenting Kenny on his song. He said, 'We sure would like to do some work with you.' So he, Leon and I went to a show lounge across the street from their office and came up with some songs. After I went back to Mercury, I told them I wanted to try something with the two of them, and out of that came *The Ice Man Cometh* album."

According to Butler, one of the songs they wrote that first day was "Never Give You Up." "That's a very interesting song from the first session after we decided we were going to work together. We recorded it at the Sound of Philadelphia Studios, but the unique thing about it was that we were locked into—by chance or by divine guidance—using my musicians instead of their studio musicians." Butler says that meant the musicians knew him and his style, and things just clicked. "Joe Tarsia, who was the engineer at the session, always talks about how we came in, my band set up their five pieces and we went in and did it in one take. Joe says, 'I remember you were on your way someplace for a gig, and you stopped in, and we did it in one take and you were gone.' We did, but one take makes you always suspect that you didn't do it well enough!" Clearly, Butler did do it well enough, as it went to #20 on the pop charts and #4 on the R&B charts, and the Gamble and Huff hit-making machine was just getting started.

Next up, and off the same album, was another Gamble, Huff and Butler composition called "Hey Western Union Man." "Kenny, Leon and I were not only the writers, but they produced, did the background vocals and just about everything that was needed," he said. "I tell people all the time that 90 percent of the arrangement was in the way Leon Huff plays piano. A lot of arrangers and orchestrators would take a word or phrase that Leon sang or played on the piano and put it in the string or horn section and end up building most of what they were doing around the way he plays the piano.

I really believe he's one of the great unsung musicians of our time. And because of Kenny's aura, I guess, he often gets overlooked in terms of his contribution to the sound of Philadelphia, but his spirit is enormous. Both Gamble and Huff cast a big shadow." The song went to #16 on the pop charts and #1 on the R&B charts in the fall of 1968.

Yet another hit from *The Ice Man Cometh* album was Butler's next release, "Only the Strong Survive." "That was a song that everybody seemed to derive their own personal meaning from—everybody heard whatever message they wanted to put into it. I went to perform at Prairie View College in Texas and this guy asked if I was going to sing it, but I really hadn't planned on it because it was a newly released song that we really hadn't worked into the act yet. He said, 'But you gotta do it.' I asked him why, and he said, 'That's the school's theme song.' So we picked our way through it to begin with, but once we started to play it, the kids just picked it up and ran with it. It was one of those things where they were singing along as opposed to listening to me sing. But it was quite complementary and was very wonderful." It was a song that many people felt strongly about, and the anthem-like nature of the song saw it go to #4 on the pop charts and #1 on the R&B charts. It was his first record to go platinum and would be recorded by Elvis Presley and Billy Paul, among others.

After the success of *The Ice Man Cometh*, which had spawned four Top 40 singles on the pop charts, all of which had made the top ten on the R&B charts, it was time for a follow-up album. Working once again with Gamble and Huff, Butler's next album was *Ice on Ice*. While it, too, generated four charting singles in 1969 and '70, only two—"Moody Woman" at #24 ("a play off of being married," Butler said) and "What's the Use of Breaking Up" at #20 ("which dealt with people who are always going through some conflict or another, and then after getting the steam out, they go back to being what they were before the pot got hot!")—made the pop Top 40. Butler says the album largely centered on "the concept of people falling in and out of love," and despite the solid writing and producing, single sales were not as good as they had been with the previous album. And though Butler was still in demand and selling records, his recording success was about to take a hit.

"After we did the first two albums, Kenny and Leon decided that they weren't going to produce any outside artists anymore and they were going to concentrate on building their own label," Butler told me. "I was under contract with Mercury and couldn't leave, so when they decided to opt out of recording outside artists, I was one of the opt-outs. I had to figure out what to do." Butler decided to start "a songwriters' workshop in Chicago

and started trying to come up with writers who could fill that void. We had a lot of success, but it wasn't necessarily for me. As a matter of fact, Natalie Cole's first two or three hits came out of guys who were involved in the workshop." In fact, while Butler would have eighteen R&B chart singles for Mercury between 1971 and 1974, none of them would make the pop Top 40. He would then sign with Motown, though with basically the same result. His career seemed to have slowed down.

"By this time, Kenny and Leon had made Philadelphia International a BIG label," he said. "They had Teddy Pendergrass, Lou Rawls and on and on. What do they need with a Jerry Butler at this point in time? But because of our relationship as friends, they said, 'Let's go back into the studio, and see if we can recapture what we did at the very beginning.' So we did. We went up to this resort up in the Pennsylvania mountains and sat down, and just started talking about just cooling out, getting away, taking a break from the routine. The idea is you need to just slow down because you're moving too fast. And that's how the song's title came about—so the song was about what it's like to 'cool out.'" Though "Cooling Out" did not make the pop charts, it did hit the R&B charts at #14 and was, of course, very big in the Carolinas. "I jokingly told one reporter that we were shooting for disco and missed! But it wound up being a very good song for shagging."

Butler continued to record until the early '80s and then became successful first in business and then as a politician in Illinois, and today he still serves as a commissioner for Cook County. He still performs, of course, and those old beach standards make up the bulk of his act. "There are some songs you can get away with not singing, but there are other songs that if you don't sing them then people don't feel that they have received their ticket's worth, so we try to do those. I try to be a good entertainer and not just a record box, so when I go to different venues I try to select the songs that I think will work best in that area. For instance, I recently did a show in the Carolinas and opened and closed with 'Cooling Out.' I did all my beach songs, and they called me back and we cooled 'em out one more time!"

It's obvious that Jerry Butler has a great love for those songs that are considered beach music and the audiences that want to hear them. "That concentration of colleges down in that area, and that love of beach music, make it a place where artists can be known and show their talent and just have a wonderful time. I don't think you'll find any region of the U.S. where the music and the people are as connected as they are to that whole beach music scene." And Jerry Butler should know; he's a star almost without parallel on both the national and beach music circuit.

The Catalinas

"Summertime's Calling Me"
1975, did not chart
Sugarbush 114

(Author's note: I have updated this entry since Carolina Beach Music: The Classic Years *was published due to a recent interview with John Barker.)*

"While driving in the mountains on the way to Appalachian State on a winter's night in 1975, I was trying to come up with an idea for a song," former Catalinas member and songwriter John Barker told the author. "Two lines—'I want to sit there in the sand, and watch those golden tans go walking by'—came to me. After trying for a while to come up with something that everyone could relate to, especially the college crowd, I came up with 'I know it isn't fair, cause you might really care, but it's different now, that summertime's callin' me.' I mean, after all, we all can't wait for the end of winter's misery and that first real summer vacation, and so I thought I had what we in the music business call a good 'hook' for a song at the very least. Well, I was driving alone but knew for certain I had to write this down. So I found a matchbook cover in the car and carefully scribbled the chorus down. I knew the rest of the story would come in time." And so on a frigid November evening, far from the coast, one of the greatest Carolina beach music classics was born. It was the song that would change the genre and start beach music on a path that would lead to more regional, beach music–specific songs. That song was Barker's matchbook composition "Summertime's Calling Me."

The Catalinas were first formed in 1958, and the lineup frequently changed, but in 1967, they recorded their first hit, "You Haven't the Right" (see *Carolina Beach Music: The Classic Years*). They recorded some other tracks on Scepter, but none were ever released, and so the group carried on, its lineup ever changing, still waiting for that hit that eluded them.

For a while, it looked like that hit might be hard to come by. Barker told me that in the early 1970s, "music was in a confused state, and some of our members were questioning our choices of direction, thinking we would fare better by adapting to the changing times. Some members even suggested that we change our name to something that sounded more contemporary, but thankfully, cooler heads prevailed. But we were struggling, always trying to find better ways to please our crowds and improve our popularity. I remember thinking at the time, 'We should stay true to our roots and try to write something that would be a hit for our beach music fans.'" He notes that "the term 'beach music' was being used more and more at the time, and there was a noticeable separation of our crowds' tastes in music. While some were going with the trends of the '70s, others, especially the fraternities and sororities, were sticking with music by the Drifters, Tams and so on. It became apparent to me that maybe the problem was there was no new beach music being written."

Though within a few years many in the industry would come to that same conclusion, Barker realized it in 1975 and wrote the first of what would become a legion of modern beach music hits—"Summertime's Calling Me." After writing those first lines and the chorus on the way up to Appalachian State, he knew he had a little more work to do, which was to "simply explain the thoughts behind the chorus." He explained the meaning behind the song's verses to the author:

> "I remember this past winter, I told myself to settle down…
> and I seriously tried to do just that."
> *(After all, things do look different in the winter, right?)*
>
> "Now here I am with everything, so beautiful and green…
> and I can't believe I told myself what I mean."
> *(Oh well, maybe I shouldn't have promised all that after all.)*

"Maybe someday soon, I can feel this way year 'round, but
it's different now and I don't want to stay in this town...
noooo."
*(I'm sure I'll grow up someday and settle down, but on second thought,
now's not that time.)*

Chorus, then horn intro again...

"I don't think I'm ready to develop a routine...when it's cold
and snow's on the ground, it's a different scene."
(Another way to say "What was I thinkin'?")

"Maybe someday soon, I can feel this way year 'round, but it's
different now and I don't want to stay in this town...noooo."

(Chorus) "I want to sit there in the sand, and watch those
golden tans go walking by."
(You know you've done this.)

"I know it isn't fair, cause you might really care, but it's different
now, that summertime's callin' me."
(Reality sets in...hope you understand...gotta go.)

Repeat chorus to end.

The group went to Reflection Studios in Charlotte to record the song,
and with Bo Shronce's strong lead, the group felt they had a winner. "We
couldn't wait til those boxes of 45s arrived at the studio," Barker said. "But
when they finally arrived, I was disappointed to see that they had misspelled
my name on that first order as 'Johnny Barke.' Of course, looking back,
if you have one of those, you have an original order record. Even I don't
have one of those." Disappointment aside, the group "started visiting radio
stations with the enthusiasm that this could really be our big break. We
were hoping our new record 'Summertime's Calling Me' would help us find
more work and make life a little easier." In an interview for *Carolina Beach
Music: The Classic Years*, Gary Barker noted, "We were really excited about it
and started performing it everywhere we went, but nothing happened and
nobody seemed interested. Finally, we even kinda quit playing it." The hope
had turned into another disappointment.

"And then something very strange happened during one of our jobs at a sorority party at Wofford College," John Barker said. "We introduced 'Summertime's Calling Me' as our latest recording and stood there amazed at what we saw next. All of the girls in the sorority lined up and performed for us while we played. Not only did they know all of the words to our song, but they had their own version of a line dance they had created for each line of the song. I remember Gary and I looking at each other in disbelief at what was going on. From that night forward, 'Summertime's Calling Me' grew quickly in popularity, mainly on college campuses in Georgia, North Carolina and South Carolina. It became an anthem for getting out of town, heading for the beach and, most of all, for having fun."

It may be cliché, but as they say, the rest is history. It was the first "new" beach song and predated other now-classic songs such as "I Love Beach Music," "Myrtle Beach Days" and "Carolina Girls." As a result, "Summertime's Calling Me" changed beach music irreversibly. Up until that time, songs that we now claim ownership of as being "beach music" were written to get air time, to sell records and, hopefully, to make the Top 40 on *national* radio. But many artists looked at the regional popularity of the record and started to write songs like it as a result, and so "Summertime's" started a new trend:

The Catalinas in the 1970s. *Courtesy of Gary Barker.*

the composition and marketing of songs about the beach *designed* to be beach music. Within a few years, bands all over the South were recording songs about beach music itself, about sitting on the beach, about summertime and any and all associated areas of beach music. "Summertime's Calling Me" started all of that.

As John Barker told me, "Time and time again, people I've never met approach me to tell me it's their favorite beach song or how much that song meant to them during their college days. Others tell me they play it over and over when they are on the way to the beach, and it starts their summer. The most rewarding compliment of all is the thought that it may have made a positive difference in someone's life. After all…life should be fun. I'm glad to say the popularity of 'Summertime's Calling Me' achieved all we had hoped for and more." I asked if there were any regrets, and he noted just one—"I wish I still had that matchbook cover!" Indeed, it was the big song on the little matchbook cover that changed beach music forever.

The Chairmen of the Board

"ON THE BEACH"
1980, did not chart
Surfside 800414

"CAROLINA GIRLS" b/w
"DOWN AT THE BEACH CLUB"
1980, did not chart
Surfside 800902

"The General always told us about this music called beach music," Chairman of the Board member Ken Knox told the author. "And I said, 'Beach music? You mean Jan and Dean and the Beach Boys?' Because coming from Detroit, that's what I'm thinking, because we had never heard beach music up there. But he said, 'We're gonna go down to the Carolinas and do this music they have called beach music. I'm going to write some songs about the culture and about all the kids going down to the beach and having a good time.'" And that's exactly what the group did. After the overwhelming national success of their music in the early 1970s, which included hits like "Give Me Just a Little More Time" and other Top 40 charters, the group headed south and created some of the most important new songs in the Carolina beach music oeuvre. For all the beach music that came before and after it, and especially in terms of the regional releases written specifically to be beach music, those

Chairmen of the Board hits that emerged in 1980 are arguably the most important songs of all. For a nationally known group to commit itself so firmly to perpetuating the genre meant that at long last, Carolina beach music had come of age.

General Norman Johnson had the distinction of performing with not one but two classic beach music acts. He was first with the Showmen, whose releases "It Will Stand" and "39-21-40 Shape" were to become beach music classics, even if they weren't big national sellers. After Johnson left the Showmen, he joined the new Invictus label formed by the famed songwriting team of Holland-Dozier-Holland, which had just left Motown. Johnson's new group, the Chairmen of the Board, consisting of Johnson and Danny Woods, Harrison Kennedy and Eddie Curtis, quickly became one of music's biggest acts, scoring hits with songs that *were* big national sellers: "Give Me Just a Little More Time" (1970, #3), "You've Got Me Dangling on a String" (1970, #38), "Everything's Tuesday" (1970, #38) and "Pay to the Piper" (1971, #13). Factoring in that Johnson had also written "Patches" by Clarence Carter (1970, #4,

The Chairmen of the Board. *Courtesy of Ken Knox.*

for which Johnson won a Grammy), "Bring the Boys Home" for Freda Payne (1971, #12) and "Want Ads" for Honey Cone (1971, #1), by the early 1970s he, and by extension the Chairmen, was considered one of the music industry's hottest properties (for more on the Showmen and the Chairmen of the Board's early hits, see *Carolina Beach Music: The Classic Years*).

But Johnson was having differences with Invictus, because after having such recognizable success as a writer and artist, he felt like he deserved a better contract and Invictus did not agree. Johnson eventually disbanded the Chairmen and pursued a solo career at Arista, but because there he didn't feel he had enough artistic control, when his contract was up he left the label. He then re-formed the Chairmen of the Board with original member Danny Woods and former backup member Ken Knox. "The Chairmen of the Board had always been one of my favorite groups," Knox said. "I used to watch them when I was in high school, and then I actually joined them in 1973 as a backup musician. You can imagine just coming out of high school and touring nationally and internationally. Then when the General put the group back together in the mid-'70s, he asked me to come up front, which was really like a dream come true." But the General had big plans, and they didn't include simply hanging around Detroit trying to live off of the Chairmen's early '70s national success; Johnson was going to take the group down to the Carolinas and immerse them in the beach music scene. "The General had always told us about beach music, but coming from Detroit I'd never even heard '39-21-40 Shape' or 'It Will Stand.' But they were records that brought the General to the attention of Holland, Dozier and Holland, and they were big down south. So he said, 'We're gonna go down to the Carolinas and I'm going to write some songs about the culture, where all the kids go down to the beach and places like the Pad.' And that's what we did." Johnson himself later said, "For the first time in eight years, I enjoyed performing music without the depression of the music business. I found an independent music industry that was still free of monopoly, politics and categorization." In 1979, Johnson and Mike Branch formed Surfside Records in an effort to revitalize a beach music industry they felt was "too dependent on old recordings." They felt that the genre couldn't survive based only on classic recordings, and so a whole new era began for the group, kicked off by 1980's "On the Beach."

"General said, 'I'm going to write a song called "On the Beach,"'" Knox told me. "He wrote 'Cool water at my feet, ice cold beer in my hand...'

The Chairmen of the Board. *Courtesy of Ken Knox.*

I mean, because that's the way it was, and that's what people were doing. The song was perfect—it gave you a scenario of what Carolina beach music was all about. That was especially true for me, because being from Detroit, I didn't know anything about beach music. But that song kind of summed it up." What Knox was initially unprepared for, however, was how well the music would be received. "Oh wow," he said. "Every time we performed the song, people would act it out—they'd toss [a drink] up, stick their hand out, you know, acting out 'ice cold beer in my hand.' The song was received very enthusiastically, but I think that was helped by the fact that when the General wrote, you could *see* everything that he was writing about. His music was very visual." The song became an instant hit in the Carolinas, and in addition to the obvious visual images in the song, there was one further element that, to this day, causes some confusion. One of the lines says, "Everybody loves to ball," and many fans seem to think this refers to one of those elements many beach music songs deal with in addition to the sand, suds and surf—sex. "No, no," Knox said. "It means everybody likes to party…it's like when the kids get away from their parents and come to the beach, they let their hair down and party til daylight. It wasn't a reference to sex."

Next up were the back-to-back hits "Carolina Girls" and "Down at the Beach Club." "Everybody had always talked about and sung about California girls, but nobody had really sung about the Carolina girls," Knox told me. "Well, the General really knew what people would like to hear about, and he said, 'I'm gonna write about the girls here.' And what the song did was to give pride to the women of the Carolinas—so much pride that you saw 'Carolina Girls, Best in the World' on license plates, T-shirts and stickers everywhere. Because of that song, every generation will be proud of the culture; being a Carolina girl means you're the best in the world." In many ways, the song was unlike any beach music song ever. It is a recognizable brand, the slogan has been on the lips of thousands and it has become a real symbol of pride in the Carolinas. People who don't know a thing about beach music, the Chairmen or much about the culture at all may well know that song, arguably the most significant work of Carolina beach music ever recorded. "A lot of other bands tell us they get requests for 'Carolina Girls,' and it's all over YouTube by many different bands. One time, General and I started researching how many versions there were, and we even found three or four rappers, black and white, doing 'Carolina Girls.' It's really been something how the song has endured."

It is almost unfortunate that the flipside held another powerful song, "Down at the Beach Club," because it certainly could have been a hit single in its own right. "General said, 'Let's do one about the beach club. If you're at the beach, you go down to the beach club, or if you're inland, you say, 'Yeah, we're going down to the beach club tonight to see the Chairmen of the Board.' The way he wrote it, you can see it, you can hear the music—and it doesn't have to be our music—you heard the music of the Tams, the Embers, the Band of Oz or whoever. The DJ was always playing beach music at the beach club, so that's where the record came from." Another beach-themed song; another Chairmen of the Board hit.

The Chairmen would go on to record a number of new beach tunes throughout the '80s and would keep right on performing until General Johnson passed away in 2010. "I feel very fortunate to have been with him for thirty-seven years. When General passed, I received probably a few thousand e-mails from people saying, 'Please keep the band going, keep the legacy going.' General's family and the fans wanted me to keep it going, and thank God they stood behind me." Today Knox carries the torch, leading the Chairmen as they sing those classics. "They are all timeless songs, and we still do them today in our show. We have to. If we don't, they'll say, 'Why don't y'all sing...' And that was the General's philosophy. If it ain't broke, don't fix it." Since it clearly "ain't broke," they go on playing some of the best beach music ever written.

Judy Clay and William Bell

"PRIVATE NUMBER"
1968, Billboard # 75
Stax 0005

S omebody had the bright idea that 'Private Number' would be a great
duet," William Bell told the author. But it wasn't meant to be a duet,
and in fact, it *actually* wasn't a duet, technically speaking, as "the two of us
were never together in the studio singing," Bell said. Yet no matter how the
end result was orchestrated, "Private Number" emerged as one of the most
soulful and heartfelt ballads in the beach music pantheon.

William Bell was born William Yarborough, and his first recordings were
as a member of the Del Rios in the late 1950s. Bell would eventually sign with
the newly formed (and renamed) Stax Records, and his first recording would
be a song he had written called "You Don't Miss Your Water." Though the
song would only reach #95 on the Billboard Hot 100, it was the beginning
of a long, productive relationship that would see Bell regarded as one of the
label's top draws and would produce a number of hits. (For more on Bell's
solo career, see the entry for "Easy Comin' Out" in this book.)

Judy Clay's (born Judy Guions) career would have a trajectory that would
parallel Bell's. Like Bell, she also started out as a member of a group,
though in this case with Lee Drinkard Warrick's famous Drinkard Singers.
Beginning when she was about fourteen, she began singing with the group,
which, at various times, would include Emily Warrick (later to be Cissy

JUDY CLAY &
WILLIAM BELL

stax

STA-0005
(ST-0019)
Pub: East
Publ. BMI
Time: 2:40

"PRIVATE NUMBER"

(B. T. Jones, William Bell)
Produced By: Booker T. Jones

STAX RECORDS 926 EAST McLEMORE MEMPHIS, TENNESSEE 38106

Houston—Whitney Houston's mother) and Dionne and Delia Warrick (later to be known as Dionne Warwick and Dee Dee Warwick). Clay would leave that group in 1960, and after moving around from label to label (including stints at Ember, Scepter and one recording with Stax) without ever having any real chart success, once she was teamed up with Billy Vera on Atlantic Records, her music at last started to sell. Though not hugely successful, 1967's "Storybook Children" went to #54 on the pop charts and #20 on the R&B charts, and the duo's 1968 release "Country Girl, City Man" went to #36 on the pop charts and #41 on the R&B charts. Clay would then return to Stax, and it was there, while recording a new album, that everything would come together at last.

"'Private Number' was a song that had been kicking around in my head for a while, and I happened to be in the studio when Judy was doing a session and she didn't have enough material," Bell told me. "Her producer asked me if I had anything that she could record. Well, this song came to mind, but I only had one verse and a chorus written. I told him I'd finish it and have it ready the next day, and Judy could record it then. Well, as luck would have it, she had to leave the next morning and go back to New York for some business. So Booker [T. Jones, of Booker T. and the MG's] and I finished up the song that night and went back into the studio and did a demo of it. On that, I sang the entire song. We sent the tapes to New York for Judy to hear so she could learn the song and then put her voice on the tapes. Somebody—it might have been Jerry Wexler—had the bright idea that this would be a great duet. They kept my verse and chorus and they put Judy on the second verse and on the choruses singing harmony with me. It turned out great and was a monumental hit for us, and it was one of the first Stax crossover pop hits." "Private Number" was a modest hit, going to #75 on the pop charts but was even bigger on the R&B charts, peaking at # 17. The song was even more successful overseas and went all the way to #8 in the UK. "It's strange when you think about it though," Bell said. "The two of us were never together in the studio singing—even though it sounds like we were—but it was a big hit. We did eventually get a chance to perform it together three or four times live on stage but never in the studio."

Clay and Bell would go on to do one more duet for Stax, 1968's "My Baby Specializes," but it would be much less successful and would only make the R&B charts. Clay would return to Atlantic for another duet with Vera and would have a few solo efforts during the next decade; only 1970's "Greatest Love," which would reach #45 on the R&B charts, was even marginally successful. She would go on to a career largely as a backup singer and then move to gospel music before dying in 2001. Bell would stay at Stax until 1974 and then sign with Mercury, where the greatest success of his career awaited him. "Trying to Love Two" peaked at #10 on the pop charts and #1 on the R&B charts, and "Easy Comin' Out (Hard Goin' In)" would climb to #30 on the R&B charts, but more importantly, it would make its mark as a major beach music classic.

Despite the fact that Bell's "Easy Comin' Out (Hard Goin' In)" is a monster beach hit, he, too, recognizes that it's his duet with Judy Clay that is the more traditional beach music hit. "We were really proud of it because it was kind of a fluke," Bell said, and oddly enough, it was this fluke, a song that wasn't supposed to be for Bell at all, nor a song for two, that has cemented itself as the greatest duet in beach music history.

Bob Collins and the Fabulous Five

"If I Didn't Have a Dime (To Play the Jukebox)"
1966, did not chart
The Jokers Three Productions 1498

W e first recorded 'If I Didn't Have a Dime' in late 1964 at Arthur Smith studios in Charlotte," Donny Trexler told the author. "But we weren't happy with the recording. We messed with it and fooled around with it, and people kept saying, 'Put that song out' when we played it live. But that first version just wasn't quite right." Two years later, however, they would get it right, and 1966's release of "If I Didn't Have a Dime" became an instant beach music classic.

Donny Trexler's first band was a group called Donny and the Blue Jets. "Then Chuck Tilley and I started a band known as the Six Teens," Trexler said. "All of us in the band were sixteen when we formed the band, but when we turned seventeen in 1960, we could still call it the Six Teens because there were six guys all in our teens." One of those Six Teens was older than the others, however, when they added Bob Collins to play drums. "At nineteen, he was three years older than us, and so when Bob turned twenty, the 'Six Teens' name was no longer accurate and we changed the name to 'Chuck Tilley and the Fabulous Five.' Chuck was the lead singer, I was the guitar player and Bob played drums." But before long, there were personnel issues within the group. Tilley left, "and we put Bob up front in January of '62. Bob did an excellent job up front and still dropped back and played drums occasionally because the drummer we hired couldn't play songs like 'Shout' and fast songs like that." The group's new name was Bob Collins and the Fabulous Five.

It wasn't long before the group discovered the song that would make them a permanent fixture in the annals of beach music history. "In 1964, we were introduced to a song by the Furys called 'If I Didn't Have a Dime,'" Trexler said. The Furys were a vocal group that had had one charting record (a remake of often-covered "Zing! Went the Strings of My Heart," which would only climb to #92 on the R&B charts in 1963) and had also done a cover of Gene Pitney's "If I Didn't Have a Dime," which was the flipside of his 1962 smash "Only Love Can Break a Heart." "But when J.D. O'Brian introduced us to the Fury's version, I really liked it, and he said, 'Donny, you can sing this song.'" The Furys' soulful version resonated with the group, and with Trexler singing lead, they decided to incorporate it into their act.

"We put it together, and the college kids really loved it," Trexler told me. "We played a lot of fraternity parties, and they always wanted to hear it. The song was so popular that we went to Arthur Smith studios in Charlotte and recorded it in late 1964, but we didn't like the recording. In the meantime, we were playing it live and people were going crazy for it. Fans were saying, 'God, you've got to record that song!' Finally, we re-recorded late in the summer of 1966 in Greensboro at Copeland Sound Studios." But after the disappointment with the first recording, they wanted to get this one right, and they knew what they needed—that raucous energy that accompanied those live performances at clubs and fraternity parties across the South. "So we took [the recording] to a club in Greensboro called the Jokers Three. We played the song and acted like we were singing it, and we got the people to carry on and we recorded the audience and the background noise. What you hear there on the song is exactly what we heard and what it sounded like when we played it [at parties and in clubs]. People went crazy over it." They felt that this element of the song was important "for the

58

people who came to see us everywhere we played, and that sound was the way it was. Our biggest fans came from places like UNC, NC State, Duke and South Carolina…there were people who would drive from Columbia all the way to the Jokers Three in Greensboro to hear us play. The fans were great, and we wanted the recording to sound the way they liked the song to sound."

Trexler jokes that when they released it early that fall, "it was an instant hit—we sold thirty copies!" But the song's popularity contributed to the group's renown and led to them playing with the Four Tops, Martha Reeves and the Vandellas, Major Lance and many other acts, some of the biggest names of the decade. "I can't name all the people we worked with in the 1960s," Trexler says. "We were the number one beach band up and down the East Coast, from Washington, D.C., south." Consequently, one would have expected them to follow that success with another recording—and they almost did. "When we recorded 'Jukebox,' we also recorded 'Lonely Drifter' by the O'Jays, and I sang that too." But the group delayed putting it out, "and Pieces of Eight released it and it hit the charts." The South Carolina–based Pieces of Eight version was released on A&M Records in 1967 and climbed to #59 on the pop charts, and after that, sensing that the group wasn't taking advantage of their opportunities or thinking big enough, Trexler says, "I decided it was time to move on." However, his association with the group wasn't over quite yet. "At that time I had written a song called 'Inventory on Heartaches.' We recorded it, and I was the arranger of the song, played guitar on it and sang backup. They went ahead and released the song because they'd gotten some money up front for it from Mainline Records. But it didn't do much back then." By that time, Trexler had joined a group called Ted Carrol and the Music Era, who had a one-off with Atlantic Records in 1968 ("What the World Needs Now Is Love"), but "that group didn't last long, so I joined the O'Kaysions." After performing with the O'Kaysions for a while, he had a band called Swing from 1972 until 1986 and then started working with his wife, Susan. Since then, Donny and Susan Trexler have gone on to be two of the biggest names in Carolina beach music, having won multiple awards and distinctions for their contributions to the industry.

Though Bob Collins and the Fabulous Five disbanded not long after Trexler left the group, today he still owns the rights to the group's name and recordings. However, despite the group's popularity in the 1960s, and while Trexler believes "the Fabulous Five has been long forgotten, unlike some of the other beach music bands of the period," he acknowledges that their recordings have taken on a new life and are now beach music favorites and huge on the Northern Soul scene. "If I Didn't Have a Dime" remains the group's greatest contribution to the genre of classic Carolina beach music, and even if it didn't sell a lot of copies when it was first released, the record's success can't be measured by initial sales but by longevity. All in all, Trexler realizes that he's associated with a beach music classic, "and I have to say I'm proud to be a part of it."

Clifford Curry

"Shag with Me"
1980, did not chart
Woodshed 001

"Shag with Me' was released when all the regional beach music songs were coming out; it was a comeback song for me," Clifford Curry told me. "I'd had a career lull after 'She Shot a Hole in My Soul,' but 'Shag with Me' brought me back. It re-energized my career and my fan base. All of a sudden I was playing more shows, radio stations were playing it and people were shagging to it everywhere." For a singer who'd had two big hits in the late 1960s, the period from 1969 to 1979 was somewhat of a dry spell. But Curry's career was sustained by his fans in the Southeast, who would welcome "Shag with Me" as one of the biggest of the new wave of regional hits about beach music and the Carolinas.

Curry's career began in Knoxville, Tennessee, when "I got my start singing with local bands," he told the author. Curry decided to go solo about 1959, but after a few unsuccessful single sides for Excello, he decided to join the Bubba Suggs Band as the featured vocalist. "It was the best band I ever played for, and we backed up Solomon Burke and Wilson Pickett and traveled on the road with Joe Tex and Little Willie John," Curry says. But performing on the road became a grind, and in 1963, "I decided to go back to Knoxville and got with a local band there, and we started playing at a club in the heart of Knoxville and the University of Tennessee. I was writing songs and doing

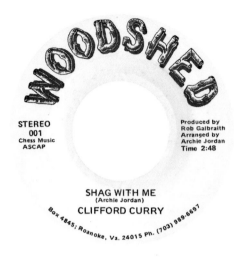

STEREO
001
Chess Music
ASCAP

Produced by
Rob Galbraith
Arranged by
Archie Jordan
Time 2:48

SHAG WITH ME
(Archie Jordan)
CLIFFORD CURRY
Box 4845; Roanoke, Va. 24015 Ph. (703) 989-6697

shows, playing every fraternity and sorority party I could."

Curry's recording career got a shot in the arm a few years later when his friend Rob Galbraith, who was a disc jockey at WNOX, let Curry use the radio station's recording equipment. Producer Buzz Cason eventually heard Curry and called Galbreath and said, "'We're going to send Clifford a couple of songs to record.' Those were 'She Shot a Hole in My Soul' and 'We're Gonna Hate Ourselves in the Morning.'" Curry and his band recorded "She Shot a Hole in My Soul" on the Bell subsidiary Elf Records. The song reached #95 on the Hot 100 and #45 on the R&B charts. The flip side of the record was "We're Gonna Hate Ourselves in the Morning," and though at the time it didn't do much, it has become a well-known song too. (Read the story of these songs in *Carolina Beach Music: The Classic Years*.) As Curry says, "I had no idea the songs were going to fit into the beach music thing like they did. I was just a singer trying to have a hit."

Suddenly, Curry was in demand in the Carolinas. He played the Williams Lake venue in Dunn, North Carolina, and then Cecil Corbett's Beach Club in Myrtle Beach. "He hired me the next weekend, Easter weekend, when the kids were out on school break. Those two weeks were the best two weeks I ever had in my career. Starting out not even knowing what beach music was, what the shag was, nothing. And that's what got me into beach music."

By 1969, however, the hits had quit coming on Elf. "I had a career lull after 'She Shot a Hole' and those songs I did with Buzz. Buzz just wasn't familiar with the whole beach music thing like I was, and we were doing things that just weren't being recognized in the Carolinas. It wasn't beach music. I was playing and writing and traveling, but the songs weren't being played." Curry recorded for several labels, generally recording a song or two at each before moving on. Without beach music audiences, however, his songs didn't seem to be catching on.

"Then my friend Archie Jordan, who had written 'What Difference You Made in My Life' for Ronnie Milsap and 'The Drifter' for Sylvia—both #1 songs on the country charts—wrote a song specifically for me." Jordan had been born in South Carolina and for a while had played guitar for the Tams. As a writer, he would write not only for Milsap and Sylvia but also Charlie Rich, Anne Murray, Barbara Mandrell and others. However, Curry says Jordan's roots were in beach music, "since he was born in South Carolina and had played with beach bands there." Jordan gave Curry a new song: "Shag with Me."

"We cut that record in 1979, and it came out on my album *Then and Now* in 1980. That was right about the time all the regional beach music songs were coming out, and it was a comeback song for me." Though the record didn't chart nationally, it did get a lot of airplay in the Carolinas. "It re-energized my career and my fan base," Curry says, "and in the Carolinas, it's as big as my earlier hits. It really is a great shag song. 'She Shot a Hole' and 'We're Gonna Hate Ourselves' are, of course, still going strong, and 'Shag with Me' is just as big in the Carolinas."

They followed "Shag with Me" a year later with another Woodshed release, "Lets Have a Party," but "Rob and those guys didn't push it the same way. It sounded and felt like 'Shag with Me'—melody-wise and dance-wise—but it didn't catch on, and it seldom got played." By this time, Jordan was out of the picture, having moved on to other projects. "We didn't really work together after that. He was mostly in Nashville writing songs." Jordan would return to his beach music roots once again, however, and in 1987 would write the Top 5 UK hit "There Ain't Nothin Like Shaggin'" for the Tams.

Even today, Curry continues to find his greatest success on the beach music circuit, churning out those beach music tunes, old and new. "I don't know, I might have another life," he says. "I'm trying not to slow down. Beach music is in my blood. They say a cat has nine lives—I hope I have nine more." Beach music lovers can only hope Clifford Curry is around for a long, long time. Odds are he has a few more hits simmering back there somewhere.

Patti Drew

"TELL HIM"
1967, Billboard #85
Capitol 5861

"WORKIN' ON A GROOVY THING"
1968, Billboard #62
Capitol 2197

Millions of listeners have no doubt heard "Workin' on a Groovy Thing"; problem is they are probably more familiar with the 5th Dimension's Top 40 version than the original by Patti Drew. Although Drew recorded a number of fine tunes, she never quite hit it big, and the stress of what was in her words a "brutal" touring schedule led her to suddenly retire from the music industry in 1971. Yet despite her limited output, she gave beach music audiences two excellent recordings in "Tell Him" and "Workin' on a Groovy Thing."

Patti Drew was born in Charleston, South Carolina, but her family moved to Evanston, Illinois, in 1956. There Patti and her sisters, Lorraine and Erma, sang in the choir at their local church. Patti's mother was a housekeeper for Maury Lathowers, the regional promotional manager for Capitol Records, and one Sunday, she asked Lathowers to come to church to hear her daughters sing. Lathowers ending up booking a formal audition for the girls, and after playing the demo for Capitol exec Peter Wright, they signed the group to a contract. Calling themselves the Drew-vels, for their first release they recorded a song Erma's husband, Carlton Black, had written. "Tell Him," with Black singing bass, was a huge regional hit in the Chicago area in 1964, though it only made it to #90 on the national R&B charts. The group released a few more singles, but having had no national success, they decided to break up.

Before long, however, Wright and Lathowers came calling again, unwilling to let Drew's magnificent voice go unutilized. "About a year after the group broke up, Peter and Maury came to me and asked me if I'd like to be a solo artist," she told Bob Abrahamian in a 2008 interview. "I didn't want to do it without the girls, [but] they wanted to be housewives and mothers. I finally said yes [and] the first thing we recorded was 'Tell Him.'" With notable singers Fontella Bass and Jackie Ross on backup, and Carlton Black singing bass once again, this time the song went to #22 on the R&B charts and #85 on the pop charts. It was a solid start for her career as a singles artist.

Drew's next charting effort was "Workin' on a Groovy Thing." Drew said she would sit around and listen to demos and try to pick good ones to record, and when she heard "Workin'" (penned by Neil Sedaka and Roger Atkins), "I thought, 'Hmm, that's a catchy little tune—I'd like to do that one.'" It was a good choice and would be Drew's biggest record, going to #34 on the R&B charts and #62 on the pop charts in 1968. It's clear Drew had a good ear for music and also clear that maybe she wasn't getting the promotion she should have; a year later, a version by the 5th Dimension that most consider inferior to Drew's would go to #20 on the pop charts.

It's always easier in retrospect to see where mistakes were made with how a singer was handled to ensure the maximum success with an audience, but today it seems there were several factors that caused Drew's career to stall at this point. First, her management didn't seem to know what kind of singer they wanted her to be. "Capitol couldn't decide if they wanted me to be another Aretha Franklin or another [jazz singer like] Nancy Wilson," she said. Secondly, perhaps as a result of not having a clear identity, she was recording the wrong types of music and a lot of cover tunes. The first single release from her second album, 1969's *I've Been Here All the Time*, was a cover of Otis Redding's "Hard to Handle" (which charted at #40 on the R&B charts), and the album also included covers of the Grass Roots' "Midnight Confessions," Ben E. King's "I Who Have Nothing" and the Drifters' "Save the Last Dance for Me." While a singer may score an occasional hit with a cover, frequently doing covers of other artists' works is generally not a recipe for recording success. Finally, Drew was on the road constantly playing the nightclub circuit—which also meant she wasn't in the studio developing new material. She was playing clubs around the country two weeks at a time, though not surprisingly, "[my act was] real big in the south." But the travel was "brutal. I lived out of a suitcase, I was always alone, I traveled by myself—It was too much." She told author Bob Pruter that she also started taking drugs and "completely lost contact with the people around me. I became militant, and finally my manager suggested I take some time off." She never went back—by 1971, she was done with the music business.

Drew admitted to Abrahamian that "sometimes I miss it, but it was too much work," so in that sense, she's glad she's out of the business. Anyone who has ever heard "Tell Him" or "Workin' on a Groovy Thing" can recognize her talent, and it seems that anyone with her exceptional voice should have been a superstar—but ultimately that was not to be. More than forty years later, however, we're left with two songs that are solid beach music classics.

The Drifters

"Kissin' in the Back Row of the Movies"
1974, did not chart
Bell 45600

"You're More than a Number (In My Little Red Book)" b/w
"Do You Have to Go Now?"
1976, did not chart
Arista 78

(Author's note: I have updated the information on "Kissin' in the Back Row" since Carolina Beach Music: The Classic Years *was published due to a recent interview with Clyde Brown.)*

You know what I remember about 'Kissin' in the Back Row'?" former Drifters co–lead singer Clyde Brown told me. "I remember that at the time I sang it I couldn't stand the song, and I didn't want to do it—I really didn't like it at all." Luckily for beach music fans everywhere, as co-lead of the Drifters, Brown did contribute his vocals to the tune, though not without some coaxing. But Brown's contributions to Drifters songs such as "Kissin' in the Back Row" and "You're More than a Number (In My Little Red Book)" during the period affectionately known as the group's "British Years" means that though their '70s hits are markedly different from the doo-wop sounds of the 1950s and the lushly orchestrated songs of the 1960s, they are among the best beach tunes recorded during the 1970s.

Clyde McPhatter left Billy Ward and the Dominoes to form the Drifters in 1953. With McPhatter singing lead, they'd have the #1 R&B hit "Money Honey" in 1953, but McPhatter was soon drafted and sold his share of the group to manager George Treadwell. Johnny Moore joined and took over as lead singer, and their first recording with Moore as lead, "Adorable," went to #1 on the R&B charts and was followed by classics such as "Ruby Baby" and "Drip Drop." However, there was tension between the group and Treadwell, and after several people were fired and Moore received his draft notice, the Drifters, it seemed, were done. But Treadwell had heard a young singer named Benjamin Nelson (later to become Ben E. King) and hired him and three members of his group the Five Crowns to become the Drifters. Their first song was "There Goes My Baby," which went to #2 on the charts and had the distinction of being the first rock record to incorporate strings. While the earlier Drifters music had more of a doo-wop feel, the new Drifters music had a more elegant sound, and the #1 hit "Save the Last Dance for Me" seemed to confirm that they'd found the right formula. But despite the group's success, King left for a solo career, and thus continued a cycle of an ever-changing lineup and the use of a variety of singers doing lead duties. Johnny Moore returned to the group and sang lead on the beach music classics "Under the Boardwalk" (#4), "I've Got Sand in My Shoes"(#33) and many others. But the Drifters, it seemed, had peaked, and 1964's "Saturday Night at the Movies" (#18), on which Moore also sang lead, was the last Top 40 American hit the group would ever have. (For a more detailed analysis of the early hits, see *Carolina Beach Music: The Classic Years*.)

Since the group's popularity was waning in the United States, in the early 1970s they headed to England, where they were bigger than ever. They signed with Bell Records, and their third release, 1973's "Like Sister and Brother," was a #7 English hit. Though Moore was still the lead singer of the group, it was around this time that Clyde Brown joined them. "I was managed by Jimmy Evans in New York City, who also managed Wilson Pickett and a number of other artists," Brown said. "Jimmy called and asked if I wanted to sing with the Drifters. At first I said I didn't know, but I met up with them in Jamaica, and later we played the London Palladium, the Middle East, South Africa, all over. Though I'd originally only signed a one-year contract, I played with them from 1974 to 1982. I really enjoyed being with the group."

Brown had signed on just in time for their fourth release on Bell, 1974's "Kissin' in the Back Row of the Movies." "It's strange though because I really didn't like that song for some reason. But Faye Treadwell [our manager at the time] said to me, 'It's gonna be a hit, Clyde—come and do the session.' I said, 'I don't like the song, and I don't feel like I can do the song justice, because I don't really like it.' She said, 'That has nothing to do with it, whether you like it or not. Go ahead and sing on it.' So I sang on it—and sure enough, it was a hit." The song went all the way to #2 in England, and the Drifters were officially back—though the record only reached #83 on the R&B charts in the United States (their last chart record of any kind in the United States). But copies could be found on jukeboxes throughout the Carolinas; beach music fans knew a good thing when they heard it.

Over the next few years, the group would record a number of hits, but the highlight in beach music circles was 1976's "You're More than a Number (In My Little Red Book)." "The song was written by Tony Macauley and Roger Greenaway, and I sang co-lead with Johnny on 'You're More than a Number,'" Brown said. "Johnny sang the hook—'You're more than a number in my little red book, you're more than a one-night date…' and so on. I sang the verses like, 'Oh baby, give us a chance/Don't let those small town rumors end our first real romance.' It was very successful in England, a top ten hit." In fact, it went all the way to #5, and the flip side, though not a chart hit, was another song beach music audiences have taken to: "Do You Have to Go Now." Perhaps because it didn't chart, Brown doesn't remember the details surrounding the making of that record. "'Do You Have to Go Now'? I really don't remember how it even goes. I still get royalties from records all the time, but I've never seen its title on the sheet. I was probably the lead singer—and if I didn't sing lead, Johnny Moore did. But I don't really remember it."

But despite the string of hits, the grind of performing was starting to get to the band. "We performed every night, and we did so many shows. We did thirty-four nights straight one time, and some of the nights we doubled. We'd sing in one town, get back on the bus and go to another town and do another show the same night. It was terrible." In addition to the constant traveling and performing, the group was also affected by the many lawsuits they had to file against all of the imitation Drifters groups. "I don't know if you know this, but we went to court about who owned the name because there were dozens of groups around the world claiming to be the Drifters. We went to court to straighten it out, but it was like opening Pandora's box. It was exhausting." With the stress of touring and litigation, Moore finally called it quits in 1978, and Brown a few years later. Nevertheless, the group has continued to go on and has continued to tour throughout the more than three decades since. There are Drifters—and imitators—even today.

As for Clyde Brown, today he performs without the Drifters. "I now have a ten-piece band, and we do a lot of corporate stuff." Brown's website lists an impressive array of jazz, pop and swing tunes that he performs but, curiously, no Drifters songs. "That's because I don't do them," he said. "I don't do the Drifters songs in my show today unless someone requests them. I do get requests for them, don't get me wrong. It's just because I choose not to do them—it's not that I don't like them. I like all of them. But I don't do them because I did them every night for so many years. Every night! So if I don't have to do them, I won't." Nevertheless, those great '70s Drifters tunes still play throughout the Carolinas, even if Brown doesn't do them as a part of his repertoire.

Donnie Elbert

"WHERE DID OUR LOVE GO?"
1971, Billboard #15
All Platinum 2330

"I CAN'T HELP MYSELF"
1972, Billboard #22
Avco 4587

In many ways, it almost seems like the fates conspired against Donnie Elbert. Despite the fact that he wrote more than one hundred songs, his two biggest hits would become chart toppers for other artists, and in both cases he would have to fight to receive his songwriting credits. As a performer, his two biggest chart recordings would be covers of Motown songs that went to #1 for other acts, with the result that he gained a reputation as more of a cover artist than an A-list performer. Yet for all that, Donnie Elbert had one of the finest falsetto voices the industry has ever heard, and his superb renditions of "Where Did Our Love Go?" and "I Can't Help Myself" have emerged as classic shaggers and favorites on the Carolina beach music scene.

When Donnie Elbert was three, his family relocated to Buffalo, New York, a move that was to have a profound influence on his future in music. In 1955, Elbert co-founded a group known as the Vibra-Harps, which also had Danny Cannon (who would later take the name Lenny O'Henry and record "Across the Street") as a member. The group would release several singles, but by 1957, Elbert left to go solo. While his first single, 1957's "What Can I Do," would make the lower reaches of the pop charts at #61, he would follow that effort with nearly thirty singles over the next thirteen years, but not one would make the American charts (one would be a big Northern Soul hit, however; 1965's "A Little Piece of Leather" would break the UK Top 30). Nevertheless, Elbert continued to write prolifically, and Motown was having a significant influence on his compositions. He wrote a song for his friend Darrell Banks called "Baby Walk Right In," and Banks would take the song, rename it and record it as "Open the Door to Your Heart" (see *Carolina Beach Music: The Classic Years*). The song would be huge for Banks, reaching #27 on the Billboard Hot 100. Elbert had finally written a hit song.

But as far as everyone but Elbert knew, he hadn't written the song at all. When the record came out, Elbert noticed that Banks, and not he, was credited with writing it. Elbert was shocked to learn that the song's rights had been given to Banks because he had told the record company that he was the composer. After a protracted legal battle, Elbert was at last able to get himself listed only as a co-writer because apparently Banks had made some minor changes, such as speeding up the tempo and changing the name. It's an indication of Banks's perfidy that while Elbert would go on to write more than one hundred songs, Banks would never again receive a songwriting credit.

In late 1966, Elbert moved to England, and after releasing several singles (1969's reggae hit "Without You" actually went to #1 in Jamaica), he moved back to the United States in 1970. His first hit back in the States was 1970's "I Can't Get Over Losing You," which climbed to #98 on the pop charts and #26 on the R&B charts, giving him his first American chart records in thirteen years. After two more releases that did not chart, he released a song he had recorded in England in 1969, a version of the Supremes' 1964 #1 hit "Where Did Our Love Go?" He offered it to a few American labels that declined it before he made a deal with the London label for release in the UK, but after the song hit #8 in England, All Platinum agreed to release it for American distribution. The song, with its rhythmic sound, went to #15 on the pop charts and sold 1.5 million records, and the bouncy beat helped it quickly become a favorite in the shag haunts of the Carolinas as well. He followed this with another Motown cover, a version of the Four Tops' #1 hit "I Can't Help Myself," because, as he said in a 1972 interview on British radio, "it's within the same pattern, and I thought it would be the best follow-up." It, too, charted, going to #22 on the pop charts and to #11 in England. The flip side, a cover of the Supremes' "Love Is Here and Now

You're Gone," may be one of the finest remakes he ever recorded, and in fact, the 45 probably sold well on the basis of the recordings on both sides. Several more chart records followed over the next few years, and while he would record more fine Motown covers, none would surpass the success of "Where Did Our Love Go?"

Unfortunately, Elbert would once again become embroiled in a songwriting credit controversy in 1975. He apparently wrote a song called "Shame, Shame, Shame" while at All Platinum, and because he was having problems with the label, he decided to take his talents elsewhere. Elbert later said that as he was shopping the song around to some English labels, All Platinum heard what he was doing and gave the song to a new group it had signed called Shirley and Company, featuring Shirley Goodman, formerly one half of the duo Shirley and Lee who had charted with 1957's "Let the Good Times Roll." "Shame, Shame, Shame" was released by Shirley and Company crediting label co-owner Sylvia Robinson as the writer, and the song went to #12 on the pop charts, #1 on the soul charts and #1 on the dance charts. Just as Darrell Banks never had another hit after recording Elbert's composition "Open the Door to Your Heart," Shirley and Company would never reach the Top 40 again either. Nevertheless, it appeared that once again Elbert had been denied the credit he deserved. Unlike the Banks case, where songwriting credit was eventually restored to Elbert, he was never legally recognized as the writer of "Shame, Shame, Shame."

After a few more releases, Elbert moved to the administrative side of the music industry as a director of A&R for Polygram's Canadian division. He would remain in that position just a few years, dying in 1989 after a stroke at the age of fifty-three. Yet despite the trouble he had receiving credit for his own work, his covers of the Motown classics "Where Did Our Love Go?" and "I Can't Help Myself" are recognized as some of the best shag songs of the early 1970s.

The Embers

"I Love Beach Music"
1979, did not chart
eEe 1002

They started calling that old rhythm and blues 'beach music' in the late '60s, because these kids would go to the beach and hear all that kind of music being played," former Embers lead singer Jackie Gore told me. "Then they'd go home and want to hear that music they heard on the beach during the summertime—that 'beach music.' Well, in 1979, we'd had a lot of young people who were following us around as we played beach music, and my wife said, 'Why don't you write a song for the young people about beach music?' So that's what I did—I sat down at my kitchen table one morning and came up with the 'I Love Beach Music' melody." And though it's hard to believe that it could have been that simple, Gore created a song that any band seeking credibility on the beach music circuit just *has* to know how to play—a song that has come to be called "the national anthem of beach music."

Teenagers Bobby Tomlinson, Jackie Gore and Blair Ellis started the original Embers back in the '50s, and they started out playing mainly rhythm and blues and soul, the type of music that would eventually become known as "beach music." After several years on the club circuit, they opened their own club in Raleigh in 1965 and then another in Atlantic Beach in 1968, and it was at that Atlantic Beach club where their career first took a real

upswing. As Bobby Tomlinson told the author, "In 1968, Archie Bell had 'Tighten Up' out with that 'dut duh duh duh duh duh' rhythm and beat to it. One night we were performing, and we were playing 'Tighten Up.' We got into a groove, just jammin', and Jackie then led right into and started singing 'Far Away Places,' and it went over. And it worked so well that we started doing it all the time." "Far Away Places" was eventually recorded on MGM and got the group their first taste of national and international recognition (read the whole story in *Carolina Beach Music: The Classic Years*). Though the single never became a big chart hit, the Embers were firmly entrenched as a credible beach music act and one of the most respected groups in the Southeast.

Over the next decade, the Embers became one of the biggest acts on the beach music circuit, and Gore decided to write "I Love Beach Music" for their younger fans. He says he figured one good way to make the song relevant was to "mention about seven or eight of the most popular beach music songs of all time. I just linked them together and made it all fit." Consequently, listeners heard references to the Dominoes' "Sixty-Minute Man," Willie Tee's "Walking Up a One Way Street," the Drifters' "Up on the Roof" and "Under the Boardwalk," the Tymes' "Ms. Grace," "39-21-40 Shape" and "It Will Stand" by the Showmen and "What Kind of Fool" by the Tams—with a few chords of the Embers' own "Far Away Places" thrown in. Perhaps most surprisingly, the song also mentioned a contemporary beach music hit, "Summertime's Calling Me," which the Catalinas had done just a few years earlier. I asked Gore if he had any reservations about mentioning another group from the Carolinas who, frankly, might be seen as competitors, but he said, "No, because they were always good friends of ours, and in fact, their piano player, Johnny Barker, started playing with the Embers not long afterwards, in 1980. He'd written 'Summertime's Calling Me' for them, and I made him real happy obviously!" So the song came out and was an instant beach music hit.

But in one of the strangest twists in the annals of beach music history, the song would find its greatest audience not as a beach music hit but as a commercial jingle in the early 1980s. "I did the song at a beach music concert," Gore said, "and instead of singing 'I Love Beach Music,' I started singing 'I Love Budweiser,' and the crowd went wild. Budweiser wanted us to record a commercial for them right then. It became a national commercial for them, and that's where the song made all of its money, through the

The Embers in the 1970s. *Courtesy of Bobby and John Tomlinson.*

association with Budweiser, not just as a song itself. It went on for a couple of years, we recorded several other commercials for Budweiser and we started playing their national events all over the country. They'd fly us all over, and that's how we made all of our money." But once the commercials stopped running, the resilience of the song really became apparent, and it became, and has remained to this day, beach music's anthem. It is probably the most recognizable song ever written about beach music, and with its ties to the old classics and standards, it serves as a bridge between the classic years and the revival years for beach music that would follow the song's release.

Though Gore is no longer with the Embers and performs today with the Legends of Beach, "I Love Beach Music" is a part of their repertoire. "I am truly not tired of singing it," Gore says. "We can stand up there and play all night long, and there won't be that much dancing. But when we play 'I Love Beach Music,' the floor fills up with people every time. The children of the people who used to come see us in the '60s and '70s are coming to see us now, and they all know the song. I'm very proud of it, very proud of what the song has done for me and my groups over the years. I never get tired of performing it." If the song's enduring popularity is any indication, Gore will be singing it for a long time to come.

The Esquires

"Get On Up"
1967, Billboard #11
Bunky 7750

"And Get Away"
1967, Billboard #22
Bunky 7752

Like many teenagers with a fondness for music, Gilbert, Alvis and Betty Moorer formed their own singing group, the Esquires. But unlike the vast majority of those groups formed in high schools across the nation in the late 1950s, the Esquires would go on to find a few moments of fame with a series of chart hits—though it would take almost a decade of laboring in obscurity until that came about.

After forming their group in 1957, the Esquires recorded "Long Hot Summer" on a local Milwaukee label with the boys backing Betty, though it received no recognition. Between 1957 and 1967, they would go through a number of personnel changes, adding and then losing Harvey Scales, adding Shawn Taylor and Sam Pace and ultimately losing Betty in 1965, who decided to go out on her own as a single artist. In 1966, the group went to Chicago to audition for Curtis Mayfield. Mayfield apparently didn't like their sound—reportedly he felt they sounded too much like the Impressions—and so they continued to line up auditions until they tried out for Bill "Bunky" Sheppard. Sheppard heard them do a song called "Get On Up" that Shawn Taylor and Gilbert Moorer had written. He liked the song, though apparently not enough to give them a record deal, and instead he had them sing backup on a series of releases by Mill Evans, none of which charted.

It was at about this time that Sheppard established his own label, Bunky Records, and for the label's first release he finally decided to issue the Esquires' "Get On Up." Arranged by Thomas Washington, who would later work with the Dells, the Chi Lites and Earth, Wind and Fire, the song was similar in content to many of the songs in the 1960s that dealt with the politics of dancing, as the vocalist implores his girl to "get on up, on the floor" and dance some of the most popular dances of the day: "We're gonna do the monkey, the Philly dog too." However, according to Mill Evans, Sheppard felt that something wasn't right about the song and called in Evans to determine what that was. "I told him, 'There's a hole there,'" Evans told Bob Pruter. "'They're singing "Get on up," and then there's a big hole there!' I worked on it and came up with the bass parts for the song. It was to fill the hole." With Evans singing that catchy bass addition, the song shot to the top of the local charts and then climbed the national charts, lodging at #11 on the pop charts and #3 on the R&B charts. Evans joined the Esquires, and they started touring the country, quickly filling seats wherever they played, including the Apollo Theater in New York. At about this time, Shawn Taylor was fired for failing to arrive on time for performances.

Now a quartet, to follow the success of their debut single, they next recorded what was—literally—a follow-up in every sense of the word. Gilbert Moorer wrote the answer record to "Get On Up," "And Get Away," and it even says "Get on up…and get away!" in the song, and it is much like its predecessor, though it is brassier. Some of the lyrics are similar, and the refrain of "Get on up" even sounds basically the same. In spite of this—or perhaps because of this—when released in 1967 it, too, performed well, reaching #9 on the R&B charts and #22 on the pop charts. Two records, two big hits. An album followed, and the future looked quite bright for the group.

But like many groups, their moment had passed, and perhaps in this case it's less difficult to fathom considering that to this point, the group had been getting by on essentially the same song. They released three more singles at Bunky in 1968, but none of them made the Top 100 of the pop charts. They then moved to Wand, where they had two more semi-successful records in 1968 and 1969, "You've Got the Power" (#91 pop, #29 R&B) and "I Don't Know" (did not chart pop, #37 R&B). They changed labels again and hit the lowest reaches of the charts on Lamarr (by this time, the Bunky label had followed the trajectory the Esquires' career seemed to be taking; by 1969, the label was defunct, its staple and principal act having been the Esquires). Eventually Evans left the group, and Shawn Taylor returned. In 1976, they released an updated version of "Get On Up" called "Get On Up '76" for Ju-Par Records. It is basically a live recording of their original with some extra verses, and some of the performance is presented differently. The song went to #62 on the R&B charts; it would be their last chart record.

Eventually the group moved back to Milwaukee and played the oldies circuit with Gilbert and Alvis Moorer as the mainstays of the group. When Gilbert Moorer passed away in 2008, the group ceased to exist, but in the hearts of beach music lovers, the Esquires' music will live forever.

The Fantastic Shakers

"Myrtle Beach Days"
1978, did not chart
The Fantastic Shakers 16256

I wrote 'Myrtle Beach Days' in 1975, and it was based on a song by Queen called 'Killer Queen,'" said Jeff Reid, "Myrtle Beach Days" songwriter and former member of the Fantastic Shakers. "It sounded a lot like 'Killer Queen,' in fact, with the piano—well actually, it didn't sound *that* good!" he said. But Reid can afford to be humble; "Myrtle Beach Days" went on to be one of the seminal songs of the new Carolina beach music era that began in the late 1970s and a bona fide beach music classic.

"In 1975, I lived in Myrtle Beach and was playing an after-hours club called the Army-Navy Club," Reid told me. "I was twenty years old and played from midnight to five in the morning. A lot of groups would come in after they finished at the clubs where they were playing, and sometimes they'd jam with us. I used to see groups like Wild Country—later known as Alabama—and the Catalinas and others come in. That's how I got to know Bo Shronce." Shronce had sung lead on the Catalinas' "Summertime's Calling Me," and on one of Shronce's visits, Reid played the Queen-like "Myrtle Beach Days" for him; as he learned later, it must have made quite an impression. Reid continued to toil away for the time being, however, "playing in part-time bands from 1975 to 1977. During that time, Bo formed a new band called Blacksmith. Well, in late 1977, he asked, 'Would you like to be in a band full time?' and I said, 'Absolutely!'" Reid joined his band, soon to be known as the Fantastic Shakers.

The Fantastic Shakers would decide to go the route of a beach band. "Because 'Summertime's Calling Me' had been out and Bo sang that, we were trying to be a beach and R&B band." But like many bands that got their start in the Carolinas, the Shakers needed that signature song that was theirs and no one else's. It would be fine to sing "Summertime's Calling Me" since Shronce was the voice that everyone knew in the lead, but realistically, that would always be a Catalinas song. They needed their own, and that's where "Myrtle Beach Days" came in. "Bo said, 'We ought to take that old song of yours, "Myrtle Beach Days," and make it a beach song,'" Reid says. Despite the fact that it was modeled after a '70s rock song, Reid says the conversion wasn't all that difficult. "As written, the chords were E to G, but after changing the chords, we decided to record it. Well, in my version I had played all the instruments, and I'd never really worked on my lead vocal—I always did keyboards, guitar, background vocals and never really worked on lead vocals much. But Bo had the right type of voice—he has a great R&B voice—so that was the right way to go, and he sang it."

With Shronce's distinctive voice singing lead, the song was a hit. "By 1980 when our album came out, it was really big," Reid says. "I think 1980 was the biggest year for beach music anyway." In fact, 1980 was the year that classics like "Carolina Girls," "On the Beach" and other local favorites came out, and also, it was when songs recorded just a bit earlier, like "Shaggin'," "I Love Beach Music," "Myrtle Beach Days" and others, were all starting to peak. Carolina beach music was hitting full stride. "I remember playing in Columbia in 1980 at the stadium, and there were six to eight thousand people there. It was quite a time." "Myrtle Beach Days" had become one of the biggest hits of the period: "I'm really proud of it," Reid says.

Reid stayed with the Shakers until 1994, when he decided to go out on his own again, filling in with different bands from time to time and recording as well. Even though he's not with the Shakers now, "when I play solo I still get asked to play 'Myrtle Beach Days' a lot. I'm glad it made the impression it made on so many people."

Friends of Distinction

"Grazing in the Grass"
1969, Billboard #3
RCA 740107

"Love or Let Me Be Lonely"
1970, Billboard #6
RCA 740319

We'd be on the road, touring, and that meant riding the bus for hours at a time," group founder Harry Elston told me. "We'd drive past pastures, cotton fields, cornfields. I'd always see these cows, just grazing, so peaceful, and I'd think to myself, 'You know, they have it made. They just graze and shit!'" Despite the uniqueness of that train of thought, Elston's observation of those moments of serenity led to the Friends of Distinction's first hit record. The result was a million-selling RIAA-certified gold record and one of two Friends of Distinction songs that beach music fans have come to love.

Harry Elston began his singing career with Ray Charles's backup band, the Hi-Fis. Eventually, the group changed their name to the Vocals and recorded for Charles's Tangerine label. None of the songs charted, and eventually the group separated. Elston told me, "Two members of the Vocals—Lamont McLemore and Marilyn McCoo—went on to form the 5th Dimension, while Floyd Butler and I went on to form the Friends of Distinction." Actually, they started as the Distinctive Friends, but after adding Barbara Love and Jessica Cleaves to complete the group, Love suggested they change the group's name to the Friends of Distinction, and it stuck.

The group next went about getting themselves a manager, and Elston said that as luck would have it, "I had a roommate named Booker Griffin, and he knew Jim Brown from back in Cleveland. When Jim came out to California for a Pro Bowl, we met and became friends. After football, when Jim embarked upon a showbiz career, I told him about our group and asked him to manage us, and he agreed. From there we did a showcase, and a lot of record companies came around and then the next day I had to go around to the different companies and pick one—you were selecting them, not the other way around. I didn't realize the enormous power I had right then, and I think about it now and laugh. I ended up choosing RCA because of a producer named John Florez and his friend Ray Cork Jr., and so we signed, selected some songs and that's how we got started."

It was at about this time that Elston drew on those experiences traveling from gig to gig, watching those cows grazing as the tour bus sped by. Hugh Masekela had recorded a #1 instrumental called "Grazing in the Grass" in 1968, and though the music was right for Elston's purposes, a vocal group needed lyrics, so Elston wrote those himself. "Well, I first called it 'Flaking in the Grass' because I didn't know I could use the same title as the instrumental since I was changing the song and adding lyrics," he said. "But everybody was like, 'Get out of here!' so I came back with the same music and title and they loved it. We recorded it at RCA for our first album, and from then things happened very quickly. We weren't teenagers, but we were pretty young, and not knowing how things worked, we just rode the wave. We didn't know until later how big the song was." With Elston singing lead, the song spent sixteen weeks on the pop charts, peaking at #3, and seventeen weeks on the R&B charts and peaked at #5. It sold more than one million copies, and the group was on its way.

Before they'd even become accustomed to the success that followed "Grazing in the Grass," they charted again with "Going in Circles," which went to #15 on the pop charts and also sold one million records. "Things were happening so fast, and we were on the road all the time, so we really didn't grasp it all until years later," Elston said. "Fortunately, our egos were intact, which is something I've always loved about our group." And while egos and success couldn't fracture the group, one joyous event did—Barbara Love was pregnant and had to take maternity leave. The group was too hot and too popular to go on extended hiatus and needed to record and tour in order to stay in the public eye. Fortunately, Elston said, "Our bass player, Stan Gilbert, said he knew a girl in Milwaukee who would be great to fill in. So, we auditioned Charlene Gibson and brought her in."

The timing was good, because "we had a song, 'Love or Let Me Be Lonely,' that had been written by Skip Scarborough, Jerry Peters and Anita Poree." Though none of the songwriters was well established at that point, Scarborough would later write hits for Earth, Wind and Fire and Bill Withers and even win a Grammy for Anita Baker's "Giving You the Best That I Got." Peters would work with Aretha Franklin, Marvin Gaye and Diana Ross and win a Grammy for co-writing "It's What I Do," and Poree would co-write songs such as "Boogie Down" and "Keep on Truckin" for Eddie Kendricks. Though those accolades would come later, the songwriters were obviously top-drawer.

"They gave us time off from touring to do an album, and we went to RCA's studio in New York and recorded 'Love or Let Me Be Lonely' there." Any doubts they may have had about Gibson's abilities were quickly dispelled, as she took lead on the song, "and she flat out tore it up," Elston said. Knowing that Love's absence could have spelled disaster for the group, Gibson's success meant they didn't miss a beat. "Charlene was a godsend," he said. "She did lead on several songs, such as 'Crazy Mary,' and she was great on them all." And never better than on "Love or Let Me Be Lonely"; it went to #6 on the pop charts and #13 on the R&B charts and was yet another smash.

But for the first time, things started to change within the group. "By then we had not revolving chairs but revolving girls," Elston said. "Barbara came back, and then Jessica split and went with Earth, Wind and Fire

The Friends of Distinction.
Courtesy of Harry Elston.

and later Parliament Funkadelic. Charlene stayed on, then she split after a couple of years too." Additionally, "being on the road was tiring, and when record sales started slipping, we felt like it was time to hang it up." Elston noted that RCA may not have really understood how to market the group either, a sentiment that Cuba Gooding of the Main Ingredient noted of his group as well (see their entry in this book). "When you are putting out maybe three or four records a year, it has to be planned. RCA didn't have many black artists, and they didn't seem to know what to do with them. You had the R&B department fighting with the pop department, because there was crossover. So we kind of got caught in the middle of that stuff, and it was political. We were lucky Jim Brown was on the scene, and so it wasn't as bad as it could have been, but it caused confusion." Ultimately, the group called it quits in 1975.

Since then, their songs have been covered by a number of artists, resulting in chart hits for the Gap Band, Luther Vandross and Paul Davis. Elston is glad that beach music audiences have taken to their music, and all in all, he's "grateful for the success we had. We weren't out there that much and for all that long before we broke up, so for our music to last this long is really a gift from God"—a sentiment no doubt shared by beach music lovers everywhere.

The Futures

"PARTY TIME MAN"
1978, did not chart
Philadelphia International 3661

If a spot on the charts is the ultimate measure of success, then the Futures certainly were not very successful. They never had a song that made the pop charts and, over the course of a decade, managed to place just a handful of singles on the R&B charts. Those weren't especially memorable, with one exception: their 1978 release, "Party Time Man," has become one of the biggest hits in beach music history. It's a remarkable accomplishment considering that, by most standards, the song was an absolute failure.

The Futures was a Philadelphia group formed in 1968, and despite some early personnel changes, the core members of the group were Frank Washington, Kenny Crew, James King and his brother John King and Henry McGilberry. Their first single was the 1970 release on Amjo "Breaking Up," which did not chart (nor did a re-release on Avalanche in 1971). They then went to Kenny Gamble and Leon Huff's Gamble Records, where they released the single "Love Is Here." Though it only went to #47 on the R&B charts in 1973, it appeared they were poised for a breakthrough under the tutelage of hit makers Gamble and Huff.

Anything ever written about the group mentions that it was at this point that they made a major, career-altering mistake. Rather than stay with Gamble and Huff, who were developing the relatively new Philadelphia

International label (home of the O'Jays, Harold Melvin and the Bluenotes and others), the group jumped to Buddah. Apparently, the group felt that the O'Jays were getting all of the label's attention, and so they left for what they thought was a better deal. Though they issued four singles at Buddah, only one charted, 1975's "Make It Last," which peaked at #35 on the R&B charts. When their contract with Buddah ended, they were without a label for several years, but in 1978, they were re-signed by Philadelphia International. The label had enough faith in them to issue their first album in 1979, *Past, Present and the Futures*, and the leadoff song was "Party Time Man." Written by Sherman Marshall (who penned "Then Came You" by the Spinners and Dionne Warwick and "Lady Love" by Lou Rawls) and Ted Wortham (writer for the Spinners, Teddy Pendergrass and Dionne Warwick), the song has that bold Philadelphia International sound, the vocals are strong and the beat was good enough that it should have been extremely popular in the clubs at the time. In fact, a longer version, running six minutes and five seconds (the original 45 ran three minutes and forty-three seconds), was released as a "disco single" for the clubs. Despite some play, it never did better than #94 on the R&B charts.

The group released another album and five further singles, but only a 1981 cover version of the Rays' 1957 hit "Silhouettes" made the R&B charts at #79. The group left Philadelphia International and broke up soon after. Eventually, McGilberry would join the Temptations, and Washington would join the Delfonics and later the Spinners, in each case to replace members who had departed.

All in all, though "Party Time Man" is not an original regionally written Carolina beach music song, it ranks right up there with songs like "Carolina Girls," "I Love Beach Music," "Summertime's Calling Me" and others as a song that any beach band worth its salt better be able to play. If you run an Internet search on the song today, you'll find it on the playlists of dozens of bands, appearing as frequently as any song in the beach music oeuvre. Perhaps because it had no national success it feels like a regional song, and maybe that's because that "Party Time" lifestyle has become a mantra for those who enjoy beach music and what it's all about. For whatever reason, few songs are more highly regarded, and as such, it holds a pretty unique position in the beach music pantheon.

Marvin Gaye

"Too Busy Thinking About My Baby"
1969, Billboard #4
Tamla 54181

"Come Get to This"
1973, Billboard #21
Tamla 54241

Although "Too Busy Thinking about My Baby" and "Come Get to This" were recorded just a few years apart, they sound different enough that they could have been recorded over a greater span of time. Each song, however, is indicative of where Marvin Gaye's career had been and where it was going. The earlier effort was one of his last recordings with that Funk Brothers–driven Motown '60s sound, while the latter was emblematic of Gaye's '70s persona, whose songs often reflected sex, seduction and sensuousness. Despite these differences, both songs have been adopted by beach music enthusiasts as popular favorites.

Marvin Gaye started his career with a later incarnation of the doo-wop group the Moonglows in 1958, which was really just a renaming of the Marquees by Moonglows founder Harvey Fuqua. Fuqua later founded his own label and signed Gaye, and eventually Berry Gordy acquired Gaye when Gordy bought out Fuqua's label. Initially, Gaye did session work and played drums on Motown recordings, but in 1961, he released several singles, which did not chart. Finally, in 1962, "Stubborn Kind of Fellow" hit #46 on the pop charts, "Hitchhike" broke the Top 40 at #30 and he was on his way at last. Over the next few years, he charted more than two dozen times, on his own and singing with Kim Weston, Mary Wells and Tammi Terrell. His last release of 1968, "I Heard It Through the Grapevine," surpassed four million in sales, was the biggest-selling song in Motown history up to that time and hit #1 on the Billboard pop, R&B and British charts.

Consequently, by the time he recorded "Too Busy Thinking About My Baby" in 1969, Gaye was one of the biggest stars in the business, but the sound of his music was definitely changing. While during the previous two years he had charted with typical Motown-sounding songs such as "If I Could Build My Whole World Around You" and "Ain't Nothing Like the Real Thing" (both duets with Terrell), his solo efforts were developing a completely different sound. In that sense, "Too Busy Thinking About My Baby" is an anachronism, and listeners can be forgiven for thinking it sounds like it should have been recorded in the mid-'60s when the more traditional Motown sound ruled the airwaves; there's a good reason for that. Actually, the song was a Norman Whitfield, Barret Strong and Janie Bradford co-written album cut that the Temptations had recorded in 1966 and that Jimmy Ruffin had also recorded but didn't release in 1967. Everything about the execution of the song follows that mid-'60s Motown sound as well. The music was by the Funk Brothers, and backing vocals were by the Andantes, who'd sung backup on classics such as Mary Wells's "My Guy," "I Can't Help Myself" by the Four Tops and some of Gaye's previous hits, such as "I'll Be Doggone," "Ain't that Peculiar" and others. With innocent lyrics based on love, not sex (i.e., "The diamonds and pearls in the world/Could never match her worth, no no/She's some kind of wonderful, people tell you/I got heaven right here on earth"), the song was clearly a throwback to simpler times. It was Gaye's second-biggest hit of the 1960s, reaching #4 on the pop charts and #1 on the R&B charts, and it was the top-selling R&B record of 1969.

It was one of the last throwback-sounding songs Gaye recorded. Soon more socially conscious songs were his forte, and by 1971, efforts such as "What's Going On," "Mercy, Mercy Me (the Ecology)" and "Inner City Blues (Make Me Want to Holler)" represented his sound. His 1973 album *Let's Get It On* went in yet another direction—sex. The sexy "Let's Get It On" went to #1, and the second single from the album was "Come Get to This." While the song is a little faster than its predecessor (giving it a good shag beat), it's easy to see it as an innocent song about a woman returning to her lover; however, it's difficult to listen to the line "I want to do something freaky to you" and interpret that as being about anything other than sex. That's apparently what audiences wanted though, as it went to #21 on the pop charts and #3 on the soul charts. Considering that the album's next single release was "You Sure Love to Ball," it's pretty clear where Gaye's music was at the time. The album became his most successful ever.

Gaye would continue to remain relevant as a singer, and his 1974 duet with Diana Ross, "My Mistake," would also become a beach music classic (see *Carolina Beach Music: The Classic Years*). Yet for all of his success, of his post-1965 hits, 1969's "Too Busy Thinking About My Baby" and 1973's "Come Get to This" best embody that beach music feel and sound.

The Georgia Prophets

"FOR THE FIRST TIME"
1969, did not chart
DoubleShot 138

"NOBODY LOVES ME LIKE YOU DO"
1970, did not chart
Capricorn 8009

"I THINK I REALLY LOVE YOU"
1971, did not chart
Together 108

It was 1969, and the Georgia Prophets appeared poised for their big break. They were fresh off the regional success of "I Got the Fever," and they had "For the First Time," another song with hit potential written all over it, recorded and ready to go. And then the major leagues came calling. "The song was offered to Motown, and Motown wanted it," Billy Scott told me. But just as it seemed that the group was about to take that next big step, a decision about money may have changed history for them. Despite the long-term success they've had in the Carolinas, one simple decision may have kept them from being the next big Motown act instead.

After Billy Scott was out of the army, he and his wife, Barbara, worked singing backup vocals in the Augusta, Georgia area. While in the studio

in June 1965, Augusta musician Tommy Witcher heard them singing and asked the two to join his band, and soon, as the Prophets, they cut two singles on Delphi, 1966's "Talk Don't Bother Me" and 1967's "Don't You Think It's Time." They got enough airplay that Jubilee picked them up, though neither charted nationally. In 1968, they landed a record deal with Smash just in time for the release of "I Got the Fever," and though the song didn't chart nationally either, it was another regional hit, and everyone could sense the group's breakthrough was imminent (see *Carolina Beach Music: The Classic Years*). They changed their name to the Georgia Prophets ("There were several other groups named the Prophets, and it was confusing for fans," Scott said), and Roy Smith, who had written "I Got the Fever," had another song for them—"For the First Time."

"Roy was an excellent songwriter, and we were really fortunate to have him to write specifically for us," Scott said. "'For the First Time' was the first duet he came up with for us, and he called up excited about the song, saying, 'I wrote you and Barbara a great song.' Well, I learned not to get too excited about songs too early because we'd been offered songs before that just weren't there. But he asked, 'Can I play some of it for you over the phone? You gotta hear it right now. You'll sing this part, Barbara sings this part, then y'all sing this part together.' So I listened, and then I got excited about it too. We'd been looking for a really good duet." It seemed they had found the song they were looking for, one that would open them up to a whole new national audience.

In order to reach that audience, "the song was offered to Motown, and Motown wanted it," Scott said. "But Tommy made all the decisions and negotiated record deals—we were just singers in the band at the time. Tommy said, 'I offered this to Motown, and they want it, but there really isn't much money in it for us.' I said, 'Okay, you're taking care of business so whatever you decide is what we'll go with.'" Instead, Witcher told them, "'I also offered it to Double Shot records out in Hollywood, and they're interested, and I think they'll be the best label for us,'" Scott says. "Well, as bad as I wanted to go with Motown at the time, we were happy with Double Shot. I got a call from Irwin Zucker, who was in charge of their promotions, and he let us know what a wonderful song it was and that he was going to do everything he could to promote it." But despite the song's potential, it didn't make the Billboard pop charts, though it did reach #36 on the Cashbox R&B charts. Zucker would later call Scott again and tell him, "'Billy, I'm just taken aback with what's happening with this song. I don't understand it, it's a turntable record.' What he meant by that was that the DJs loved the song, but it didn't sell like he wanted it to. Of course we were really disappointed because we knew that it was a great tune." Perhaps in retrospect, while Double Shot was a fine label, it was much smaller than Motown and perhaps Motown could have promoted the record better; no one will ever know.

As the 1970s began, Witcher decided that the Georgia Prophets might need to add another female vocalist, so he decided to hire Janet Helm. Janet came to the group, and she brought a song she'd written with her called "California," which would go on to be one of the greatest beach music classics of all time. Though they were now signed with Capricorn, Scott felt that "unfortunately Capricorn was most interested in promoting their southern rock groups like the Allman Brothers, and so ['California'] wasn't promoted much nationally" (see *Carolina Beach Music: The Classic Years*). But it was as big regionally, and the group was experiencing unprecedented levels of popularity.

By then, "Roy had to start writing songs for three people—me, Barbara *and* Janet—as opposed to writing just for a solo artist or duet," Scott said, "but he was excited about the possibilities because he had heard what we'd just done on 'California.'" Smith next wrote "Nobody Loves Me Like You Do," and "Janet helped us with vocal arrangements. Coming off of two hits like 'For the First Time' and 'California,' we were very much in demand in the Southeast, and the songs helped because the compatibility of the three voices after 'California' was just phenomenal," Scott

says. "'Nobody Loves Me Like You Do' was what it was because of that third voice, because of Janet." Scott notes that in fact they liked the finished product so much that "we decided to have the horn and string arranger come back and put strings on 'Don't You Think It's Time,' which had been released originally in 1967, so we used it on the flip side."

Even though they were coming off a string of national single releases and regional hits, the group was splintering, and Scott said he, Barbara and Janet felt like they were moving in one direction and the rest of the group was going in another. Ultimately, Scott, Barbara and Janet started their own group in 1971. Witcher owned the rights to the Georgia Prophets name, but Scott, Barbara and Janet "didn't want to lose the name Prophets and lose our identity, so we went with the Three Prophets." But not only did they have to change their name, they also had to look for a backup band. "We had hired this little four-piece band out of Rock Hill to back us up," Scott says, "and they were more rock-and-roll than R&B. But they came to us one day and said, 'We've got a song we wrote.' I thought that, being rock-and-rollers, they couldn't write anything we could use, but I said, 'Let me listen to it sometime.' Well, we were on the road, and they called me to their room and played 'I Think I Really Love You' for me. I liked it and agreed we needed to record it, and so we went to a studio and put it on tape. I had a friend named Roy Callaway, and when I played it for him, he said, 'The production's not good enough on this thing, nor is the arrangement,' but he was involved with an Atlanta outfit called Together Records. Together was excited about the song, so we went in and recorded it, and Janet came up with a vocal arrangement that was awesome." Scott said that to his surprise, however, "the song did absolutely nothing! But that song was one of the best songs I think we recorded."

Nevertheless, Together Records apparently felt good enough about the group that they wanted an album. They said, "You've got a lot of good material, and we've got a good producer, so let's record an album." The producer they'd hired was Norman Whitfield, who had produced and co-written a number of Motown hits, such as "Ain't Too Proud to Beg," "I Heard It Through the Grapevine," "War" and many others. "We were really excited," Scott said. "We had an album deal, a well-known producer, everything was great. Then two to three weeks before production, the FBI charged the owner of the company with racketeering and murder. They shut the record company down, and that cut our legs right out from under us. Nothing happened after that. That was our last opportunity for an album."

The Three Prophets. *Courtesy of Billy Scott.*

Despite the fact that they missed out on what might have been their best shot at chart success, the group's music has remained a mainstay of the beach music circuit, and those songs are probably as popular today as ever. "I just got an e-mail from Korea a few weeks ago, and they want to reissue

the only Georgia Prophets album that was put out by Tommy Witcher,"
Scott said. This album with 'Nobody Loves Me Like You Do,' 'I Got the
Fever,' 'California' and 'For the First Time' will be reissued in Korea and
Japan, so I'm real excited about that." Proof, of course, that even today,
whether the music is credited to the Prophets, the Georgia Prophets or the
Three Prophets, those harmonious sounds and solid beach music tracks are
as big as ever.

Jimmy Gilstrap

"SWING YOUR DADDY"
1975, Billboard #55
Roxbury 2006

It's an honor to know that people still listen to 'Swing Your Daddy,'" Jim Gilstrap told the author. "I'm so appreciative of [beach music audiences] who keep the music alive because the industry has changed so much." And though Gilstrap is very modest and genuinely appreciative, his is one of the most famous and well-known voices of all the artists on this survey—even if you don't always know it's his voice you're hearing. From the theme to television's *Good Times*, to the Peter Pan Peanut Butter jingle, to his work with Stevie Wonder, Michael Jackson, Dolly Parton and others, Gilstrap's career as a session vocalist and backup singer is unparalleled. Yet it is his own single effort, 1975's "Swing Your Daddy," for which beach music aficionados know him best.

"When I first started singing, I had a manager named Bumps Blackwell, and Bumps was working with Sam Cooke," Gilstrap said. "In 1964, my group was called the Duprells, and though we were in high school here, we were signed to sing backup for Sam Cooke on tour. Well, the night before we were supposed to leave, I was walking home from a party and I saw a police and the coroner's people rolling a body on a gurney out of a motel on Ninety-second and Figueroa. The next morning, I'd packed my bags and walked fifteen blocks to another singer's house, waiting to be picked up

to go on tour. Bumps called us and said, 'We're not going anywhere, Sam got killed last night,' and I flashed back and thought, 'Oh, no, that was his body I saw,' and sure enough it was. We'd only been with Sam about a month before he passed."

Despite the professional setback that the cancellation of the tour meant for Gilstrap's career, he moved on to other, even bigger opportunities. "I was with a group called the Doodletown Pipers, and we used to do the *Ed Sullivan Show*, we did the Frontier Hotel in Vegas six months a year and we opened for acts like the Supremes. Later I started working with Stevie Wonder, and we were actually roommates for a couple of years in Queens." It was when he was working with Wonder that one of his most famous vocal contributions came about and put him in a position where listeners everywhere heard his work—even if they weren't aware it was him. "We were at Jimi Hendrix's Electric Lady Studios in the Village, and it was about three o'clock in the morning when we recorded 'You Are the Sunshine of My Life.' Stevie asked me to sing the opening lines, and my girlfriend at the time, Lani Groves, sang the next few lines." The song went all the way to #1 and netted Wonder a Grammy. In gratitude, he also gave Gilstrap a gold record for his efforts. Gilstrap would later work on both *Talking Book* and *Inversions*, two of Wonder's most highly acclaimed albums.

With nearly a decade of experience behind him, Gilstrap was ready to go out on his own by the mid-1970s, and opportunity came knocking. "A friend of mine named Carolyn Willis was in the group Honey Cone," he said. "She called me one day and said they were looking for a singer over at Chelsea Records. The guy who ran the company was Wes Farrell, who was married to Tina Sinatra, and the company was doing really well. So I went over and they signed me, and then they brought me 'Swing Your Daddy' to record." "Swing Your Daddy" was written by Kenny Nolan, who'd written #1 songs such as "My Eyes Adored You" for Frankie Valli and "Lady Marmalade" for LaBelle already that year and would later write and sing his own song, "I Like Dreamin'," which went to #3 in 1977. Gilstrap knew it was a good opportunity for him, and the label thought it had the potential to be a hit as well. "They brought the song in and told me they wanted an Eddie Kendricks/Smokey Robinson kind of sound. So I did it, but I honestly did not expect it to do what it did. It was big all over Europe—I even went to England and did *Top of the Pops*—and it was in the Top 10 on the R&B charts here in the States. But the record did what it did due to Kenny Nolan, because he also produced it and even sang background on it too."

Though the record peaked at #55 on the pop charts in 1975, Gilstrap seemed poised to make a big breakout, but a miscalculation may have caused his career to lose the momentum it had gained. "Then we did an

Jim Gilstrap. *Courtesy of Jim Gilstrap.*

album called *Love Talk*," he said. "I really had no input as far as what they put on the album cover, and unfortunately they put a nude couple, back-to-back, on the front of the album. Well, back in those days, they wouldn't even put the album in stores in some parts of the country, and so it didn't sell. By the time they revamped the album and put a picture of me on the cover, the album had played itself out."

By that point, Gilstrap was getting tired of some aspects of being a headline act, however. "After *Love Talk*, I got away from solo recording. It had been a lot of fun, and I got to know a lot of the artists at Chelsea, and 'Swing Your Daddy' had been a real blessing. But I started to do some other things." Indeed, Gilstrap built one of the most impressive résumés of anyone in the recording industry. During his years as an artist in a supporting role, he has worked with Quincy Jones, the Temptations, the Four Tops, Barbra Streisand, Rod Stewart, Whitney Houston, Dolly Parton and Michael Jackson on the *Thriller* and *Off the Wall* albums. He has done movie vocals on films such as *Grease*, *The Matrix* and *Rocky* and television work on *Cheers*, *The Simpsons* and, of course, as the singer on the well-known theme for *Good Times*, where his voice sings "Temporary layoffs…Ain't we lucky we got 'em—Good Times!" "The royalties for that alone have paid very, very well," he told me.

Far too often it seems artists have a big moment or two as performers and then spend the rest of their careers looking for that next hit, and they're sometimes eternally bitter that things haven't perhaps worked out as expected. Not so with Jim Gilstrap, a successful man who says, "I have had fun working throughout the industry—it's been a wonderful career. And I feel blessed that even today people such as beach music fans remember 'Swing Your Daddy.' It's a real honor to be doing this interview." Considering he has worked with some of the biggest names in the business, from Sam Cooke to Michael Jackson, Jim Gilstrap is truly a humble man.

Hot Chocolate

"It Started with a Kiss"
1982, did not chart
RAK 344

While most music lovers in the United States know Hot Chocolate for a handful of songs they recorded in the 1970s, in England they are regarded as one of the biggest recording acts of all time. There they racked up twenty-five Top 40 records and were one of only three acts (with Diana Ross and Elvis Presley) to have at least one chart record every year during the 1970s; in fact, they charted at least once for fifteen straight years. One of those hits, "It Started with a Kiss," was a Top 5 hit in England, but surprisingly, it didn't chart at all in the United States. Nevertheless, beach music lovers have found something appealing about the song, and it has remained a beach music standard almost since its release.

Hot Chocolate founder Errol Brown was born in Jamaica, though it was his teenage years growing up in England that would serve as the spark that would ignite his musical career. Although he had no aspirations to sing professionally, he told Tony Lewis of *Blues and Soul* that after his mother died, "I began to get these words and melodies in my head, which I think may have come from the shock of all that. So, while I was hanging out with these guys, I'd start humming and singing along to these melodies… one day one of them—Tony Wilson—said, 'You have these melodies that

I think are very catchy. Would you like to write songs?'...And that's how I started...It was like I'd suddenly discovered what I was meant to do."

The guys formed a group known as the Hot Chocolate Band, and for their first song, they called on Brown's Jamaican roots and "reggae-fied" John Lennon's "Give Peace a Chance," only to discover that in order to change the lyrics they had to have Lennon's permission. To their surprise, Lennon liked the song, and the Beatles' Apple Label decided to sign them as a result. They released the single in 1969, and though it got some airplay, it did not chart. Apple Records soon folded, so the group went to the RAK label, where the multiracial group now simply called Hot Chocolate consisted of Brown and Wilson as well as Harvey Hinsley, Larry Ferguson, Patrick Olive and Tony Connor. Their 1970 release, "Love Is Life," hit #6 on the British charts, and while they went on to have a number of hits in England (including 1973's "Brother Louie," which when released by the group Stories in the United States shot to #1), it wasn't until 1974 that the group would finally find American success when "Emma" went to #8 in the United States. Other American hits would follow, including "You Sexy Thing" (1975, #3), "So You Win Again" (1977, #31) and "Every One's a Winner" (1978, #6), their last U.S. Top 40 hit.

In 1982, "It Started with a Kiss" once again drew on Brown's childhood for inspiration. Brown said his first crush had been especially memorable to him, and so when writing the song he wrote it about "my first puppy-love at school in Jamaica. You know, when you don't have a solid family base that does impact your emotional character. Plus, with all the calypso music I heard early on in Jamaica being very story-orientated stuff, I think some of my [songs] did reflect that story-telling element." Brown was even more specific about the song with the *Mail On Sunday*, and he said, "I thought of the title and connected it to my puppy love for a girl in my class in Jamaica when I was nine. Her name was Barbara Blackwood. She would have no idea it had anything to do with her." The song tells the story of a boy whose childhood romance starts "with a kiss in the back row of a classroom," up through the teenage years when he "couldn't help but notice that new distant look in your eyes...I couldn't hold on to your love, I couldn't hold on to my dream." Later he encounters her on the street: "I heard my voice cry out your name as you looked then looked away/I felt so hurt." Certainly, it's a relatable song, with its subject matter about first love and the times one wonders, "What if things had turned out differently?"

In England, the song went to #5 in 1982, was re-released in 1992 and went to #31 and was re-released yet again in 1998 and went to #18. In fact, in a 2004 poll, English listeners ranked it as one of the Top 20 love songs of all time. In America, while it did not chart, by the mid-1980s it had started to be established as a favorite on the Carolina beach music scene—as it is today.

By the time the song was released in 1982, Brown was tiring of the grind of touring and performing. He told Lewis, "I realized that I was coming to the end of my creativeness. From about '81 on, I'd been struggling to write and couldn't come up with anything. I felt tired, and I felt—rightly or wrongly—that everything was on my shoulders. You know, the other members of the band were happy to relax and enjoy their lives, while I was struggling and striving to come up with something. I felt it was too much pressure, and overall I just felt that I'd done my thing…it just wasn't fun anymore. So I left." Brown went on to a solo career, and on a personal level, he later had the distinction of receiving an MBE (Most Excellent Order of the British Empire) for his services in British music, as well as the Ivor Novello Award for Outstanding Contribution to British Music.

Brown has now retired and lives in the Bahamas, although most of the other original members of the group continue to perform without him. Yet despite the fact that Brown has called it quits, "It Started with a Kiss" lives on throughout the Carolinas, playing out its timeless tale of that first boyhood crush.

Millie Jackson

"Ask Me What You Want"
1972, Billboard #27
Spring 123

"My Man, a Sweet Man"
1972, Billboard #42
Spring 127

You know, to me it was just a nothing song," Millie Jackson said of her 1972 hit, "My Man, a Sweet Man," and her opinion of "Ask Me What You Want," another great shag tune, isn't much better. Perhaps that shouldn't surprise music lovers, because Jackson has never been one to give the expected answer to a question. Though she has released more than sixty singles, only two have made the Billboard Top 40, and in some cases, it's because doing things her way resulted in recordings that couldn't be played on conventional radio without being heavily censored. But Jackson has always been an iconoclast, even when it meant forgoing the financial security that would have come from doing things the way everybody else does them. This rebelliousness even extends as far as the mainstream music she did record early in her career, and so perhaps it should come as no shock that these two songs, now regarded as beach music classics, were not songs she cared much for at all.

As a teenager, Millie Jackson ran away from home and ended up living in New York. For a while she worked as a model, but her life would change when in 1964 she was out in a Harlem nightclub and on a dare she took the stage after claiming she could sing better than the act being paid to perform. The club owner was so impressed with her performance that he hired her that night. For the next few years, she worked singing in bars throughout the area before finally recording a single on MGM ("A Little Bit of Something") that didn't chart. She next signed with Spring Records, a small label whose biggest acts were Little Eva and Joe Simon.

Her first Spring release was 1971's "A Child of God," which bubbled under at #102 on the pop charts and went to #22 on the R&B charts. Her next release was a song she co-wrote with Billy Nichols, "Ask Me What You Want." The song is an excellent slice of early '70s soul boosted by Jackson's strong voice. However, like much of her early music, she dismisses it today. In an interview for TV One's program *Unsung*, she said, "It's just some lyrics put to a Motown groove. I didn't feel that song at all…it's just a huge lie, one of the biggest lies I ever sang in my life. You can tell I was not in control of my career at the time." Apparently, those in control of her career knew what the public wanted, however, and it would be her second-biggest hit, peaking at #27 on the pop charts and #4 on the R&B charts.

Her next release was 1972's "My Man, a Sweet Man." Now a beach music and Northern Soul favorite, the song has been re-pressed over the years alternately as "My Man's a Sweet Man" and "My Man Is a Sweet Man." No matter what the name, it's also a song Jackson dismisses today, and even at the time, she was aware she didn't want a career singing songs like it—despite the success she was having. "I couldn't picture me singing 'My man is a sweet man/my man is a kind man/I know he's a fine man/ and he's mine all mine' [forever]. Who cares?" Jackson apparently felt that the pop/soul sound about adoring relationships just wasn't the type of music she wanted to be known for. "You know, to me it was just a nothing song," she said. "I mean, who walks around and says 'My man is a sweet man/my man is a kind man/my man is a fine man/ he's mine, mine, mine.'…And the person next to you is going, 'So?'" Yet despite her own misgivings about the subject matter of the song, once again the public was appeased, and the catchy single went to #42 on the pop charts, #7 on the R&B charts and #50 in England, making it her first transatlantic hit.

Jackson continued to have success. In 1973, "It Hurts So Good" would not only be featured in the film *Cleopatra Jones*, but it would also be the biggest chart hit of her career, going to #24 on the pop charts and #3 on the R&B charts. "If Loving You Is Wrong I Don't Want to Be Right" would also perform well, going to #42 in 1975 and earning two Grammy nominations, and the album it was on, *Caught Up*, would earn a gold record. Yet Jackson still wasn't really happy with the work she was producing. "A gold record didn't mean too much to me because I found out it wasn't gold, it was just gold colored," she told TV One. "I couldn't pawn it."

Ironically, it was the success of this mainstream music that she didn't like that allowed her to finally take control of her career. By the late '70s, she was recording more risqué material with increasingly provocative titles. The 1977 album *Feeling Bitchy* was the first to cross the line, and later albums such as *Back to the S__t*, featuring a cover picture of Jackson sitting on the toilet, saw her branded as a very adult, sexually explicit singer—a reputation she has done much to foster and nothing to dispel.

It's probably not surprising that the further she's moved from the mainstream, the less chart success she has had. Perhaps what is most unfortunate is that based on those early '70s singles, it appears that Jackson could have been a solid R&B performer in the mold of Gladys Knight (to whom she has often been compared) had she chosen to stay with mainstream music. If "Ask Me What You Want" and "My Man, a Sweet Man" are any indication, perhaps her alternate path was beach music's loss.

Janice

"I Told You So"
1975, did not chart
Fantasy 748

We wrote 'I Told You So' in twelve minutes," Janice Barnett told me. "We didn't sit down and plan to write it or anything—it just came out. And it surprised us how much people loved it because we didn't expect it. We'd worked for years writing songs, and then 'I Told You So' almost wrote itself and it becomes our anthem. Its reception truly amazed us, but we still sing it to this day."

Janice Barnett was a teenage beauty queen and *Jet Magazine* model, but her dream was to make it as a singer. That dream began to come true when she became the lead singer for Reggie Saddler's band, which would work under a variety of names in the late '60s and early 1970s, including Janice and the Jammers. Though they recorded several singles on the Dee-Lite label, none charted, and the group seemed destined for a career as an opening act for better-known groups. It was in fact after one such opening act in 1971 that Tina Turner called Janice and asked her to join the Ikettes as a backup singer. "She called me in North Carolina when I was at home, and my dad heard the conversation. Well, he had a fit! He said, 'You will not work for that pimp Ike Turner! He's nothing but a drug addict, and he beats up on his wife. You're not going to work for him. I'm not going to kill him over my daughter.' I cried, and I was

disappointed, but I obeyed my father and I'm glad I did."

Instead, by 1974, she and Saddler were married and they decided to head to California. "I always wanted to be a singer, and I begged Reggie to take me to California. We agreed that if in thirty days if nothing happened we'd come home and go back and do gigs on weekends and be satisfied with our life as it was. But I told him I had always wanted more than that, and I had dreamed of it all my life and I just wanted to take a chance." Saddler had faith in his wife, so they took their savings and headed out to California.

Despite every effort to make contacts and connections there, when thirty days were up, it appeared that the dream was over. "We had been around to a lot of places and nothing had happened, and so it was time to come home. We'd already left when I realized I'd forgotten my coat, so we went back to get it." When they returned to the building where she had left her coat, she walked in and "who's sitting there but Richard Pryor. I was stunned. I started talking a hundred miles an hour, telling him how I'd come from North Carolina and how all I wanted was a chance, and then I looked at him and saw he was just looking at me—he hadn't said a thing. Then he did the craziest thing; he looked at me and looked down at my open-toed shoes. Not at my face, or hair, or anything else, just at my feet, and said, 'Damn, you got some pretty feet!' I looked at him like he was crazy."

But Pryor was clearly taken with her and told her to come with him. They walked down the street to a bar, and even though she didn't drink and didn't go to bars, she decided to go inside anyway. Pryor bought drinks all around, shook hands and talked with pretty much everyone there—except Janice. "I started to think about what I'd done coming into the bar, and I started to get embarrassed and then I got mad," Janice said. "Finally, I jumped up and started walking back to the car as fast as I could, thinking, 'I'm sick of this. I'll go back home and milk my daddy's cows.' I heard this voice say, 'Hey!' and I kept on walking—I was mad as a hornet." Suddenly Pryor grabbed her. "'Where are you going?' he asked me. I stuck my finger in his face and said, 'Let me tell you one thing, you knew it took a lot for me to ask you to give me a chance, and then you take me to some bar and leave me standing there waiting on you like some twit. But somebody helped you once, somebody gave you a break. You didn't have to sit there and make me feel like a beggar.'" He walked me to the car and asked the band, 'Does this belong to you?' And they all kind of shook their heads like, 'We know her, and we know how she is when she gets mad!'" Pryor thought a moment and told them, "Come with me."

Prior took the group to a club called the Total Experience and told them to get ready for an audition. "When we came out, we were standing in front of the Soul Train logo—it was their headquarters—and we had a private audience with the cast and crew as they were practicing for the show," Janice said. "Then Richard stuck his finger in my face—now I wouldn't say this or use language like this, but I think you need to hear what was really said—and he said, 'I'll tell you one thing, bitch, you better be able to sing!' Well, we brought that house down. But when we finished, they said nothing. They were looking at us, they didn't clap, they didn't do anything. But even though they said nothing, I knew we had done our best and I went to the dressing room in tears. I ripped off my top—I tore it up—I was so frustrated. Then all of a sudden we heard this beating sound, and it was like they were in shock and didn't recover until we were off stage. 'Encore! Encore!' They wanted us back!"

Janice said there was a problem with going back, however: "I had torn up my clothes! So I pulled out a scarf, wrapped it up around my breasts and around my neck—it's the only way I could go back outside!—and we got out there and they went nuts." Their encore convinced the audience that the group was for real, and that led to Pryor's friend Joe Hubbard becoming their manager. He tried to add a little polish to the girl from North Carolina who had worn pigtails not long before. "They changed the color of my hair, and they tried to give me speech therapy. They gave up because they said, 'She's never gonna change, leave her alone, you might mess up her voice. Let her be who she is. We can't take her to charm school—she's just a country girl!'" Janice said, laughing.

The group soon came under the tutelage of Harvey Fuqua, who had developed talent at Motown, including the Spinners and Marvin Gaye. Fuqua was also developing acts for Fantasy Records in Los Angeles, and struck by Janice's strong voice, he suggested the group call themselves simply "Janice." Fuqua decided the group needed to put together an album, and so they went into the studio to record. "We were in the studio at the top of the RCA building with Marvin Gaye and a couple of other people like Smokey

Robinson who were always around Harvey. We were just playing around, and Reggie started playing something on the guitar, and when he did, I started putting lyrics to it and so did he. Harvey heard us and said, 'What's that you're messing with? What are you working on?' We played it for him, and he really liked it. That song became 'I Told You So.'

"It's funny. We had all these songs we'd worked on for years, and this one we wrote in just twelve minutes went on to become our signature song," Barnett told me. "We didn't sit down and plan to write it or anything. It just came out. It was just Reggie and me going back and forth talking about how our relationship had developed. 'I told you, didn't I, that I was going to be your wife'—there we were playing around with each other and that kind of thing." Even though the song wasn't originally supposed to be on the album, "Harvey was an old Motown veteran, and he always tested the records. The test audience loved it, so we put it on the album." And though the song never charted, live audiences have always loved it. "Everybody liked 'Wake Up Smiling' and 'Goody Two Shoes,' but 'I Told You So' was the one they really went nuts for. It just amazed us how people loved it—how the women sang it and how it brought people together and how we could see the love in the room."

Unfortunately, while their 1975 album sold well in some areas of the country, neither it nor the single releases was ever a big hit. Fuqua moved on to other projects, and while the group played clubs for many years, eventually Janice and Reggie divorced and the group came apart. Janice went on to do both television and stage work, and eventually she turned to the ministry while also continuing to work in beach music, recording and performing duets with notables such as Maurice Williams and Billy Scott. Her association with beach music led to her winning a beach music award as female vocalist of the year, as half of duo of the year (with Billy Scott), and her induction into the Beach Music Hall of Fame. Ultimately, these awards and a number of other nominations led to her being hailed as the "Queen of Beach Music." I asked her why she was given that name, and she said, "I used to wonder that too. I asked and was told that it was because I started out as teenager and as a female singing in a man's arena, and that opened the door for other women in Carolina beach music."

Long after he helped her get her big break, Janice saw Richard Pryor again and asked him why he'd never asked her for anything in return. "He told me something that has really helped me. He said, 'Just help somebody else the way I did you, with no strings attached.' And I been giving back through the ministry ever since." Beach music has obviously been a big part of that giving back too, for another reason. "For me, the beach music community was family; beach music was not just about music—for me, beach music was about friends. They were people I grew up with, we had our babies together, we told each other our problems. They're the people that I love and that loved me. It was never just about the music. What more can I say?"

Jay and the Techniques

"Apples, Peaches, Pumpkin Pie"
1967, Billboard #6
Smash 2086

"Keep the Ball Rollin'"
1967, Billboard #14
Smash 2124

I didn't like 'Apples, Peaches, Pumpkin Pie,'" Jay and the Techniques' lead singer Jay Proctor told me. "I'm a very soulful singer, and there wasn't any soul in that song at all. I didn't want to sing about no damn fruit!" Yet despite his disdain for the song, "Apples, Peaches, Pumpkin Pie" and its follow-up, "Keep the Ball Rollin'," were two of 1967's biggest hits and were very popular in the shag clubs of the Carolinas as well.

Jay Proctor was an Allentown, Pennsylvania singer who had cut a few unsuccessful singles in 1960 and '61 and who, by the mid-'60s, was still trying to find direction with his musical career. Proctor told me that he and his friend George "Lucky" Lloyd were "sitting in a bar having a beer when a friend of ours came in and said he was starting a group, and he asked us to audition. We tried out in groups, and there was one white guy and three black guys trying out in my group and each of us took a turn singing a song. Well, when the white guy got through with his song, and it was time for our songs, he said, 'It ain't right for a white guy to be in the background,'

Jay and the Techniques. *Courtesy of Jay Proctor.*

so I kicked him out. It wasn't my house or my group, and I just took over. I started kicking everybody out so only the ones I wanted were there—I was kicking people out left and right! But that's how we ended with the seven guys we ended up with." By the time the dust had settled, Proctor and Lloyd had teamed with Chuck Crowl, Karl Landis, Ronnie Goosley, Jon Walsh and Dante Dancho and had formed the Techniques.

In 1966, the group came to the attention of Philadelphia producer Jerry Ross, who was riding a string of pop-star discoveries such as Dee Dee Warwick, Keith, Spanky and Our Gang and Bobby Hebb. Ross had offered Hebb a song called "Apples, Peaches, Pumpkin Pie" as a follow-up to his smash "Sunny," but Hebb refused it, and Ross gave it to his new group instead. "Actually, several people and groups had tried recording the song—I think even Jerry Butler," Proctor said. "Jerry Ross didn't like the way any of them did it, and so he gave it to me. I'm raw off the street, I don't know anything about music, so I just opened my mouth and whatever came out, came out. Well, whatever came out pleased him, so we got to release it." The "we" in this case comes with a qualifier, because Proctor was the only member of the group to actually attend the recording session. "Jerry used session musicians on everything we did. The band was the road group, and they never went in the studio. I asked Jerry to use them, but he just felt they weren't good enough because they didn't read music well." But to his credit, Ross chose top-notch session musicians and singers, including backup singers who would later go on to have their own hits: Melba Moore and Nick Ashford and Valerie Simpson.

In addition to not being allowed in the studio, when the record was released the band was in for another surprise: the record's label said it was by *Jay and* the Techniques, though they simply considered themselves the Techniques. "I think Jerry changed it because there was Smokey Robinson and the Miracles, and Martha and the Vandellas, and he just didn't like that single-name thing. It wasn't that I was the leader of the group, just the lead singer on the song. Then it didn't make sense to change it back after the song was a hit." And the song was indeed a hit. It went to #6 on the pop charts, sold one million copies and earned a gold record—a phenomenal debut effort by anyone's estimation. So despite the fact that the group hadn't actually played on the song, and their name had been changed without their being asked, and even though Proctor says he "didn't even like the song," since it was a hit the group just shrugged it all off. "The rest of the group wished they could have played on it, but early on it wasn't a problem— though I think it became a problem later on when some of them got jealous and things like that."

They were to face yet another more serious crisis soon enough, however. "They had drafted a whole bunch of my guys as soon as the first record came out," Proctor told me. "There was a woman who was the head of the draft board in Allentown whose son went into the army, and she was pissed because we didn't go in. She had the guys drafted out of anger, and she didn't even know us. But the governor invited me to come see him, and he told me, 'As long as you guys stay together, you'll never have to go into the army.'" The governor was true to his promise, and, crisis averted, Proctor headed back to the studio to record their next hit.

"'Keep the Ball Rollin'" was written just for us," Proctor said. "But Jerry Ross picked the song. I didn't pick anything, and I didn't do anything but go in and perform what I was told or asked to. But I wasn't crazy about 'Keep the Ball Rollin'' either—that wasn't soulful to me. But of course I did it, and I'm glad I did." Ross clearly had a better ear for a hit than his lead singer, as "Keep the Ball Rollin'" soared to #14 on the charts, sold one million copies and earned them yet another gold record.

Their next recording, "Strawberry Shortcake," was by the same writers who had composed "Apples, Peaches" and sounded so much like it that "we never did it live but once because it was too close to 'Apples, Peaches.' It was by the same writers, used the same musicians, same singer. It was okay, and it had a nice beat, but those kinds of songs, you hear them once and you don't want to hear them no more." "Strawberry" peaked at #30, and after just one more Top 100 record in 1968, the group's charting days were over as quickly as they had begun. "The music was all way too bubble-gummy—they even called it bubble gum soul. You look back at it, and it was kind of ridiculous," Proctor said. "It was way far from what I thought my career would be like. I never really had the chance to do anything soulful like I wanted to do." Perhaps it was inevitable that with Proctor being the sole focus of the group—and with Proctor himself unhappy about the music they were offered—before long, dissension started to set in and they broke up. He notes that when they split up, their deferment deal with the governor was voided, "and [the other guys in the group] were drafted. That's a true story."

Eventually Proctor re-formed the group with new members, and though they released a few singles in the '70s, nothing really connected with audiences. Proctor continues to perform and plays the beach music circuit as well. "I've been to the Carolinas, and my producer is real hot on beach music. And I'll tell you, I appreciate what they do in the Carolinas. They like to shag—they shagged me to death when I was there! But God bless 'em, I enjoy being down there and it's refreshing to see it." That includes playing those two songs he really didn't like all that much at first, songs that still resonate with lovers of classic beach music even today.

Robert Knight

"Everlasting Love"
1967, Billboard #13
Rising Sons 705

E verlasting Love' was a difficult song to sing because it was hard to sing a fast song slow," Robert Knight told the author. "But I didn't sing it the way they had written it, and instead I made some changes to fit my voice." The result was a song that made the highest reaches of both the pop and R&B charts, was a stunning success and has gone on to be one of the most often-covered songs of all time. It's a beach music classic, as well.

Tennessee-born Robert Peebles started his musical career as a member of the Paramounts. That group signed a contract with Dot Records, and "we made a little noise with 'When You Dance' and 'Why Do You Have to Go.'" The group wasn't terribly successful, so their producer, Noel Ball, "convinced me to go out as a solo act," Knight said. Ball also had him change his name to Robert Knight "because disc jockeys were always pronouncing my name wrong, saying 'Pebbles' and things like that," Knight said. Though technically still a member of the Paramounts, Ball had him record some solo sides, of which 1962's "Free Me" was the most noteworthy. Despite claims today that the group broke their contract with Dot and was prevented from recording for several years, Knight says this was not true (though it is true that neither the group nor Knight could have recorded for anyone *other than* Dot at the time) and that the group broke up while Knight continued to work on a degree in chemistry at Tennessee State University and later at Vanderbilt. While in school, he formed another group, the Fairlanes, not with the intention of recording but simply "because I met these guys and we started singing—everybody was singing on street corners then." But by the time Knight finished his degree, he had been "discovered" once again while singing in a nightclub.

"Buzz Cason had worked for Noel Ball, and Buzz was working with Mac Gayden. Cason was starting his new Rising Sons label and working on some material with Mac," Knight said. They approached Knight about signing with them and put together a few tunes for him to record. In his autobiography, Cason said the idea behind "Everlasting Love" (its name taken from Jeremiah 31.3, which says, "Yea, I have loved you with an everlasting love") was to do a Motown-type song, and Cason and Gayden cobbled together some material they already had to complete the song. It didn't get a lot of thought because it was going to be used as the flip side of a track called "The Weeper," and in fact, Knight wouldn't have access to the completed version of the song until the actual recording session. And

Robert Knight. *Courtesy of Robert Knight.*

Knight was fully aware of the song's shortcomings. "Buzz and Mac were country artists, and I was R&B, and so I had to make it more of an R&B song," Knight said. "I practiced and practiced on it—it was a hard song to sing because at the time it was hard to sing a fast song slow. I didn't sing it the way they had written it. I made some changes to fit my voice, and I didn't do it note for note. They had the melody going too fast, and it was jamming, it wasn't doing right, it wasn't sounding right. So I started what you call a steady step. I start singing a beat and a half: 'hearts-go-a-stray'—like that. It wasn't like that in the beginning, and I think that's what got 'Everlasting Love' off the ground."

Even with the completed product, Knight wasn't convinced it was a great song, nor was anyone else. He thought "Everlasting Love" was supposed to be the B-side and thought the song that was eventually released as the record's B-side ("The Weeper" had been shelved and was never released), "Somebody's Baby," was better: "It was a good R&B song, and I think I did a better job on it!" But Knight says that "somebody turned it over and started playing 'Everlasting Love,' and that's what we went with." As a result, the record that was twice destined to be a B-side before being flipped would be a classic. "Everlasting Love" would go to #13 on the Billboard pop charts during its twelve-week run, and it would also reach #14 on the R&B charts. Unfortunately, its follow-up, "Blessed Are the Lonely," would barely crack the charts at #97, and only one more of Knight's records, 1968's "Isn't It Lonely Together," would chart, and it simply duplicated the marginal success of its predecessor (#97). It was Knight's last chart record in this country.

Knight would go on to be very successful in England on the Northern Soul scene, however, and when re-released in 1973, his 1968 effort "Love on a Mountain Top" was a major UK hit. That prompted a re-release of "Everlasting Love" in England, and though it had originally only gone to #40 in 1968, in 1974 it went all the way to #19. Covers of "Everlasting Love" by other artists have been popular as well, with Love Affair's version going to #1 in England in 1968, while versions by Carl Carlton, Rex Smith and Rachel Sweet, Gloria Estefan and others have all performed well. It is one of only two songs to reach the U.S. Top 40 in the 1960s, '70s, '80s and '90s.

By the mid-1970s, Knight had moved away from recording, but unlike many artists, he had a career and a college education to fall back on. He went on to work at Vanderbilt University as a chemical lab technician and worked there until he retired just a few years ago. He still performs and is "working on an album with Cason and Gayden now," though he says it is a long way from being finished. Like his close friend Clifford Curry, he is

Robert Knight. *Courtesy of Robert Knight.*

aware of his music's popularity on the beach music scene and is always eager to perform in the Carolinas. Perhaps his future efforts will yield another song as much-appreciated as the beach music classic "Everlasting Love" as well.

Major Lance

"You're Everything I Need"
1975, did not chart
Osiris 001

With one of the most distinctive voices on the Chicago soul scene and a half dozen Top 40 hits, Major Lance hit the highest of highs as a '60s soul singer. Though there would be few hits after the 1960s, later in his career he would still produce one big beach music hit in 1975's "You're Everything I Need." Unfortunately, it would be his last chart record of any type before a downward spiral that resulted in a prison sentence for selling cocaine and a series of heart attacks that would kill him at age fifty-five.

"Major" was actually Lance's given name when he was born in Mississippi in 1939. His family moved to Chicago, where he attended Wells High School along with soul greats Jerry Butler and Curtis Mayfield, and Mayfield would in fact go on to have a significant impact on his career. After appearances with several soul groups, including the Five Gospel Harmonaires and the Floats, he had a single release for Mercury titled "I Got a Girl." Despite being penned by old schoolmate Mayfield, the single failed to chart, and heading into the 1960s, Lance was just another talented singer in search of a break.

Okeh Records apparently felt Lance had something to offer, and though his first single stiffed when released in 1962, his next release, a song Mayfield had written, "The Monkey Time," would be an enormous hit. Actually,

Gene Chandler, who had taken "Duke of Earl" to #1 in 1962, wanted the song and reportedly even had his dance steps down and was ready to perform it as well as sing it. However, Mayfield held firm and gave the song to Lance. Backed by the Chicago group the Artistics, who would have their own big beach music hit a few years later with "I'm Gonna Miss You," "The Monkey Time" went to #8 on the Billboard chart and #2 on the R&B charts, and suddenly Lance was a star. His next release, "Hey Little Girl," went to #13 on the pop charts, followed by 1964's "Um, Um, Um, Um, Um, Um," which went to #5 and climbed to #1 on the R&B charts. Both were also written by Mayfield.

Lance had nearly a dozen chart hits over the next few years, but of his Top 40 chart records, only one was not written by Mayfield. When Mayfield moved on to focus on his own group, the Impressions, Lance's records stopped charting. Like Jan Bradley, whose hit "Mama Didn't Lie" was also written by Mayfield (see *Carolina Beach Music: The Classic Years*), Lance just couldn't seem to land a hit without Mayfield, and he never again had a Top 40 record after 1965.

Lance's last single for Okeh was in 1968, and though he recorded singles for several labels thereafter, none was immensely successful. Lance moved to England for a few years, where he saw a resurgence in popularity due to the burgeoning Northern Soul scene before moving back to the United States. He formed his own record label with friend Al Jackson, the great drummer for Booker T. and the M.G.s, who was a songwriter and producer in his own right. For the label's first release, they decided to record a song Frederick Knight had written, "You're Everything I Need." Though Knight's biggest hit would come a few years later with Anita Ward's #1 smash "Ring My Bell," the smooth soulful sound of "You're Everything I Need" was a good tune for Lance's vocal range, and with its updated instrumentation it had more of a '70s sound than Lance's earlier work. Unfortunately, though, audiences didn't connect with the record, and although it did reach #50 on the R&B charts, it failed to make the pop charts at

all; it would sadly be Lance's last chart record of any type in this country. Lance would release one more record on Osiris, 1975's "I've Got a Right to Cry," but before Osiris really had a chance to establish itself, Al Jackson was murdered in his Memphis home, and without his partner, Lance was forced to fold the label that same year.

Lance would only record two singles between 1976 and 1978, and neither charted. His career was clearly faltering, and this was exacerbated by his arrest for cocaine possession in 1978, which led to a three-year prison sentence. Though he would record a few singles after his release from prison, his recording days were essentially over, and after a heart attack in 1987, his career as a live performer was over as well. In 1994, he died of heart disease, his body obviously weakened by his years of drug abuse.

Despite the fact that Lance had a great deal of early success with songs like "The Monkey Time" and a later career marred by controversy, sandwiched in the middle was a great '70s beach song in "You're Everything I Need." Though not a big hit, the song was interesting enough that Brenton Wood would also record it in 1977. Nonetheless, it's Lance's little-known 1975 version that offers an updated beach music sound and a departure from the classic sound of his earlier career.

Little Frankie

"I WANT TO MARRY YOU"
1967, did not chart
Smash 2067

My career was supposed to have been boxing," Roy C. Hammond, aka Little Frankie, told me. "I planned to be the heavyweight champion of the world, and I trained like hell." That training would come to naught, but perhaps that was a good thing; maybe Roy C. Hammond would have been just another fighter, but he has been anything but just another singer. He has recorded more than three dozen singles and a dozen albums, and before that, as a member of the Genies, he recorded more than a half dozen more. Oddly enough though, despite having chart records both as a member of the Genies and as Roy C., it is a one-off, non-charting record under a name that was not even his own that most appeals to beach music lovers: his 1967 single as Little Frankie, "I Want to Marry You."

Roy C. Hammond was born in Georgia, but "I went to New York when I was fourteen years old." He says he was bitten by the boxing bug early on and trained to be a professional fighter. "I was about sixteen years old, and I was working with Freddy Brown and Whitey Bimstein, who'd worked with Joe Louis. We were at Stillman's Gym, not far from Madison Square Garden. There was a fighter there named Hurricane Jackson, who'd fought and lost to Floyd Patterson," Hammond said. "Well, I had a chance to fight with him, but since he saw me as just a kid he told me, 'You can hit me

as hard as you want, and I won't hit you back.' I thought that was great, and so I got in the ring with him." Considering that at one time or another, Stillman's Gym had seen or would see the likes of fighters such as Joe Louis, Jersey Joe Walcott, Rocky Graziano and Sugar Ray Robinson, every day people flocked to the gym hoping to catch a glimpse of the stars and future stars of boxing. Consequently, "people would pay to see boxers train, so there were about one hundred or so people there that day," Hammond said. "I threw a punch, and because he thought I was just a kid, he wasn't expecting it to be what it was, and it really shook him up. But I'd been training for some time, and it connected. But he'd promised, he said he wasn't going to hit me, right? And so I wasn't expecting it and 'Bam'—right in the face. Tears started coming in my eyes, and I said, 'I'm getting out of here right now.'" Hammond's fighting career was officially over.

"So I quit that day. And on the way back to Long Beach, Long Island, where I lived, I took the train and I'm walking through the train station singing when one of the guys from the group the Genies heard me and came over and asked if I was interested in singing with them. They needed a tenor, and that was something I knew I could do." So Hammond joined the group, "and we would hang out and sing on the boardwalk in Long Beach. There'd be big crowds on Friday and Saturday night, and that's how we met Bob Shad." Shad was an A&R man for Mercury who liked the group's sound and signed them to a contract. What they didn't know was that Shad had started his own label—"we thought we were signing with Mercury"—but after he signed them they learned that their music was coming out on his new Shad label. "We were only there for one record," Hammond says, but that record was 1959's "Who's That Knocking?" which the group took to #71 on the Billboard charts.

The single got them noticed, and "we left Shad and went to Atlantic. Jerry Wexler auditioned us, and Claude Johnson, our lead singer, did about fourteen songs for him. Mr. Wexler didn't like any of them, and he asked me if I had anything. I did one and—bam!—he said, 'I'll take that one.'

127

I did another, and he said, 'I'll take that one too.' Well, by the time it was over, Claude Johnson quit. He said he didn't want to sing background, that he wasn't born to sing in the background. So the group broke up, and those recordings were never released." Hammond notes that Johnson may have been on to something, however, because he joined Roland Trone and the two of them, as Don and Juan, had the #7 smash hit "What's Your Name" in 1962. "I guess that proved he didn't have to sing in the background!" Hammond said.

Eventually Hammond went solo and, recording as Roy C., scored with the classic "Shotgun Wedding," which went to #14 on the R&B charts in 1965. Like many '60s soul recordings, it was even bigger in England, going to #6 on the singles chart and then again to #8 when re-released in 1972. The single spawned his first album, 1966's *That Shotgun Wedding Man*, and so at this point, Hammond's career was really starting to take off. He was writing songs and even managing an act, and that's when 1967's "I Want to Marry You" came about.

Hammond had written "I Want to Marry You," but it wasn't for him. "What happened was that there was a singer known as Little Frankie, who I was planning to record. We were in the studio, and he just couldn't sing the song." Hammond became frustrated, and eventually, "I just stepped up to the mike, and I did the song. I did the singing. I was his manager, and I'd written it, so when he couldn't get it right, I did it instead. I just took over." The recording came off, and the airplay got enough of a response that audiences wanted to hear it live. Hammond and the real Little Frankie thought they had it worked out so Little Frankie could perform it on stage, but the first time he was scheduled to sing it live, there was a problem again. "After I did it in the studio, I really hoped he could pick it up on the shows, but he couldn't do that either. We did a show in Philadelphia with Charlie Brown, and Little Frankie came out on stage and he blew it. He couldn't perform. He was nervous and messed up in front of 1,700 people." So, Hammond said, "after that, for a while I just took the name Little Frankie." He, and not the original Little Frankie, sang the song in live performances, and though the song didn't chart, it was popular nevertheless. But despite its popularity, Hammond had no interest in continuing to perform as Little Frankie. "After that I dropped the name, because I didn't want to continue using two names. For audiences it would be too confusing."

Hammond went on to record several dozen more singles over the years on several labels, and in the 1970s, he'd make the R&B charts with singles such as "Got to Get Enough," "Don't Blame the Man" and "Love Me til

Tomorrow Comes." In 1973, his album *Sex & Soul* also made the R&B charts, and each of the more than a dozen subsequent albums had a loyal following as well. He later formed his own label and moved his headquarters to Allendale, South Carolina, roughly thirty miles from where he was born. He produced an album by Dennis Edwards of the Temptations, among others, and in 1998 his song "Love Me, Love Me" was sampled in a song on the soundtrack of *How Stella Got Her Groove Back*. He's still working today and not just doing his old material either.

Yet from his days with the Genies to his many recordings as Roy C., for beach music lovers, it is his turn as Little Frankie singing "I Want to Marry You" that has gained him immortality. As for it being loved by the beach music crowd, he said, "It's a great thing any time music is recognized anywhere. It's something that I did in the field of not-really-hardcore R&B, and thank God, somebody liked it!"

The Main Ingredient

"Everybody Plays the Fool"
1972, Billboard #3
RCA 74-0731

"Just Don't Want to Be Lonely"
1974, Billboard #10
RCA 0205

Everybody Plays the Fool' was actually written for Charlie Pride," Main Ingredient lead singer Cuba Gooding told me. "I took it to him, he listened to it and decided it wasn't country enough for him to sing. He said, 'I'll never be able to sell this as a country song. It's more like a pop song.' So we gave it to our arranger, put an orchestra behind it and recorded it ourselves. But we never liked it—we never believed 'Everybody Plays the Fool' was going to be a hit record." But the record surprised them all, becoming the group's first big hit and the first of two great songs by the Main Ingredient destined to become beach music classics.

The Main Ingredient was a Harlem group that began as the Poets (*not* the Poets that sang the beach classic "She Blew a Good Thing") and consisted of Donald McPherson, Luther Simmons and Tony Silvester. Even though Gooding wasn't an original member of the group, he was friends with the guys, and they all came from similar backgrounds. "If you were a kid growing up in Harlem, and you didn't want to be a pimp or a bum or a gangster, and you weren't well educated, you sang or hoped to be in the music business," Gooding said. "I grew up eight blocks from the Apollo Theater, and at that time I could walk down 125th Street and run into Sammy Davis Jr., Ella Fitzgerald, Sam Cooke, Jackie Wilson and that ilk. We believed it was the entertainment capital of the world." The group, without Gooding at that point, first recorded on the Red Bird label, later changed their name to the Insiders and then in 1967 released two singles on RCA. They then changed their name to the Main Ingredient (taken from the wording on a Coke bottle) and, from 1969 to 1971, released nine more singles. Several of these records made the lower reaches of the charts, but none were big Billboard pop hits.

Gooding had been singing backup with the group occasionally, after working for a while "as a door-to-door salesman selling encyclopedias and magazines." But even when he performed with the group, "it was never promoted as four Main Ingredients. We had a theory as to how to do music. Three singers in front, and if a fourth or fifth note was necessary to fill up the harmony, use the musicians, use instruments to do the fourth or fifth note—'stacked harmony' with only three actual voices but two or three people in the background singing harmony at the same time. Financially it was more comfortable to spread the payroll between three people rather than five people with five families to feed and splitting the money five ways." However, Gooding's role was about to change, as McPherson contracted leukemia and died not long afterward. "I would have never been able to join the group if Donald had lived," Gooding said, and he was elevated to the role of lead singer. But Gooding's distinctive voice meant a new sound—and success the likes of which the group had not previously seen.

First up was "Everybody Plays the Fool," and after Charlie Pride passed on the song, "we gave it to our arranger, put an orchestra behind it and recorded it. But we never liked it—we never believed it was going to be a hit record. We wanted to be more like the Temptations or the Four Tops, and that's what the rest of our album was about. But they sent us on a European tour for two weeks, and when we came back 'Everybody Plays the Fool' was the hottest record on pop radio." Oddly enough, the group, which until that time had been firmly entrenched as an R&B group, at first couldn't get airplay for it on soul stations. "Black stations wouldn't even play it. They said it wasn't R&B. RCA signed me to a three-year contract as the lead singer for the group, everybody was rolling in dough because of the song, but the black stations wouldn't play it." Eventually that would change, of course, and the song sold more than one million copies, was awarded with a gold record and was nominated for a Grammy as best R&B song of the year.

The group released three more moderately charting singles before their next big hit, 1974's "Just Don't Want to Be Lonely." "The song had been recorded by three or four artists before we did it," Gooding said. "Blue Magic did a good version, and Ronnie Dyson did it and almost had a hit record with it [#60 on the pop charts]...Well, we were on the road as usual going to a gig on what used to be called the chitlin circuit, and we turned on the radio and someone was singing it—maybe Blue Magic. And we said, 'Let's put that on the next album.'" But the group wasn't content to merely imitate the other groups—and wasn't sure that would work anyway. "'Just Don't Want to Be Lonely' was always done as a slow ballad," Gooding says, "and it always crashed and burned. When we put the grooves on it, like at the beginning—'dum-dum, dah dah dumm dum...'—it just took off." It went to #8 on the R&B chart and #10 on the pop chart, sold over one million copies and even charted in England, going to #27.

Their next few singles did moderately well but were not big hits, and 1975's "Rolling Down a Mountainside" was their next release. "It was another one we adapted," Gooding said. "It was done by Isaac Hayes as a ballad, but we put a 'dah daha daha' groove to it and it did well." Despite its success on the R&B charts (#7), the song didn't do well on the pop charts (#92). Though they would have seven or eight more songs make the R&B charts, "Rolling Down a Mountainside" would be their last pop charter.

Perhaps it was just as well, as members of the group were ready to move on to other projects and, in some cases, pursue single careers, though they separated and came back together several times. Gooding now performs those classic hits all over the country, and eventually he discovered how popular his music was on the beach music circuit. "Beach music is very near and dear to my heart," he says. "When O.C. Smith was alive, I was part of a team of entertainers who were promoting beach music down in Myrtle Beach. I also did an album produced by Charles Wallert, who also produced 'Brenda' for O.C. So we all went down there and were performing continually and thought we'd put a tour together to take beach music all

132

over the world, but because O.C. died and other things happened, it fell by the wayside." But Gooding appreciates beach music and how the love for classic music keeps a special part of this country's musical history vibrant. "It wasn't so much about the songs themselves but the treatment we gave the songs. The music today—hip-hop, rap—puts the emphasis on everything except the actual voice. Disco, rock—the emphasis wasn't on the voice at all." But Gooding knows that beach music lovers appreciate the music for all the right reasons, and even though today he may be even better known as the father of Oscar winner Cuba Gooding Jr. ("The media decided to put the senior after my name after he won the Oscar—that was never my plan"), he is still known to beach music enthusiasts as the lead on two beach music classics.

Jackie Moore

"SWEET CHARLIE BABE"
1973, Billboard #42
Atlantic 2956

"BOTH ENDS AGAINST THE MIDDLE"
1973, Billboard #102
Atlantic 2989

Looking at Jackie Moore's body of work, it seems unbelievable that she had just one Top 40 pop hit, that being 1970's "Precious, Precious." Despite the fact that the Top 40 pop charts didn't give her her due, beach music enthusiasts certainly have, as both "Sweet Charlie Babe" and "Both Ends Against the Middle" are major beach music hits.

Jackie Moore got her start in Jacksonville, Florida, and in 1968, she moved to Philadelphia. Her first recording there was "Dear John," which was released on the Shout label but debuted to little fanfare. A second single on Shout in 1968, and one on Wand in 1969, appeared with much the same results. At this point, she went to Atlantic Records in New York, where her first release was the 1970 single "Willpower." That song failed to generate much play, but after it was released, someone (reportedly a hometown DJ in Jacksonville) flipped the record to the B-side and started playing "Precious, Precious." Within the next few months, that B-side had climbed to #30 on the pop charts and #12 on the R&B charts and had sold more than one

million records; it was awarded a gold record in March 1971. Jackie Moore was at last on her way.

It seems hard to believe that someone as obviously talented as Moore, hot on the heels of a million seller, could fail to find an audience on the pop charts, but that is exactly what happened. Four singles on Atlantic followed, but none cracked the Billboard pop Hot 100. Perhaps Atlantic didn't know how to market her to a crossover market, although at the same time they *were* doing a good job with the Spinners, Roberta Flack and Aretha Franklin. But Moore's records weren't selling to pop audiences, and perhaps to discover that something her records seemed to lack, they sent her back to Philadelphia to record at Sigma Sound Studios where the great Philadelphia International soul sounds of the '70s would be recorded.

The move seemed to pay off. "Sweet Charlie Babe," a song written by Phil Hurtt (who wrote the Spinners' "I'll Be Around" that same year) and Bunny Sigler (who wrote several songs for the O'Jays), had a far more sophisticated sound than some of her earlier efforts. Though it probably should have been a solid Top 40 hit, it stalled at #42. The very next release was "Both Ends Against the Middle," which was co-written by Hurtt and Tony Bell. This song had a bouncy, clean feel that categorized so many of the tracks that were popular in England on the Northern Soul scene, but it did no better than "bubble under" the Top 100 at #102. Despite the fact that neither of these releases was terribly impressive chart-wise (though both did well on the R&B charts), Atlantic did release an album called *Sweet Charlie Babe*, Moore's first album. The album basically contained the A- and B-sides of every one of her singles up to that point, going all the way back three years to "Precious, Precious"; "Sweet Charlie Babe" led off side one, and "Both Ends" led off side two. The album did not do well, no doubt because the expanse of time represented different directions in her music, multiple producers and songwriters and no cohesion whatsoever. Besides, anyone who had bought her singles didn't need to buy the album—there were no unreleased songs on it. In this case, it was pretty clear Atlantic dropped the ball.

By this time, no doubt, Moore and Atlantic had envisioned greater success than they had had, and Moore left the label. By 1975, she was on the Kayvette label, where her first release there was a big R&B chart hit, "Make Me Feel Like a Woman." None of the five Kayvette singles she released did anything on the pop charts, though all made the R&B charts. By 1978, she had moved to Columbia, and her first release there was a very fine song, "Personally," which Karla Bonoff would cover and take to #19 on the pop charts in 1982. Not only did this song not make the pop charts, it only went to #92 on the R&B charts. An album followed, as did several singles; her last R&B chart hit was in 1983, and no new releases have appeared since the 1990s.

With her strong voice and some really excellent releases, it is very hard to believe Jackie Moore didn't have more success on the charts. But beach music audiences have a way of taking songs that didn't do all that well and giving them a new life. At least in the Carolinas they have been appreciated as the quality cuts that they are.

The Poets

"She Blew a Good Thing"
1966, Billboard #45
Symbol 214

When working on *Carolina Beach Music: The Classic Years*, perhaps the song I most regretted omitting was the Poets' "She Blew a Good Thing." It would have to be considered one of the best beach tunes of all time, yet when writing that volume I could find almost nothing about the song, the group or their recordings, and consequently I omitted them. Very little additional information has come to light since then; it is easier to find out information about who they were not than who they were.

The Poets who sang "She Blew a Good Thing" were Ronnie Lewis, Melvin Bradford, Paul Fulton and Johnny James, a Brooklyn-based group that would eventually sign with Charleston, South Carolina–born Henry "Juggy Murray" Jones's Symbol Records in New York. Although Fulton had been the bass singer with the Chips of "Rubber Biscuit" fame and would also sing with the Invitations, Blue Chips and the Velours, the rest of the group doesn't seem to have had extensive experience in the industry. In 1966, the Poets would release three singles on Symbol, and the first, "She Blew a Good Thing," co-written by Ronnie Lewis and Murray, was their only chart record, topping out at #45 on the pop charts and #2 on the R&B charts. Another well-loved song along the Carolina coast was "So Young (and So Innocent)," though it did not chart. After their third 1966 release, "I'm

Particular," a *Billboard* magazine article of May 28, 1966, says the group followed with a tour of Baltimore, Pittsburgh, Memphis, Richmond and other venues, to culminate in an appearance at the Apollo Theater in New York. But after those three 1966 releases and the tour, it seems the group simply dissolved.

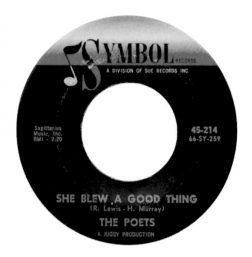

The song was released in England as by the American Poets, to avoid confusion with another Poets group from England. Further adding to the confusion was that there was also another American group known as the Poets that cut one single on Flash, and this Los Angeles–based group consisted of Roy Ayers, James Bedford, Sherman Clark, Robert Griffett and Frederick Nance. *Another* Poets group from New York was recording on Lieber and Stoller's Red Bird label. Tony Silvester, Luther Simmons and Donald McPherson would eventually change their name to the Insiders and later re-emerge as the Main Ingredient. After McPherson's death in 1971, they would add Cuba Gooding and would go on to have hits such as "Just Don't Want to Be Lonely" and "Everybody Plays the Fool" (see the entry for the Main Ingredient elsewhere in this book). None of these groups were the Poets that recorded "She Blew a Good Thing," however, though they have often been confused. In short, other than some superficial information about the group and the song, much about their identity is still a mystery—and, after the passage of almost fifty years, is likely to remain so.

James and Bobby Purify

"I'm Your Puppet"
1966, Billboard #6
Bell 648

"Wish You Didn't Have to Go"
1967, Billboard #38
Bell 660

"Let Love Come Between Us"
1967, Billboard #23
Bell 685

Although in *The Heart of Rock and Roll* Dave Marsh calls them "a minor league version of Sam and Dave," with eight singles on the pop charts in the late 1960s (compared to Sam and Dave's thirteen), and considering that "I'm Your Puppet" was a Top 10 hit a full year before Sam and Dave made it into the Top 10 with "Soul Man," James and Bobby Purify were hardly imitators nor "minor league." And while perhaps it is true that only a handful of their songs come to mind today, their music has been filling dance floors for decades.

James Purify and Robert Lee Dickey were cousins, and one weekend in 1963, Robert dropped by a club to see James's group, the Dothan Sextet, perform. As luck would have it, the group's guitarist quit that very night, and Dickey joined them on stage to help them fulfill their contract. From then on, he was a permanent member of the group, and by 1965, they were touring with and backing up the likes of Otis Redding, Wilson Pickett and James Brown. At an August 1966 performance in Pensacola, Florida, producer "Papa Don" Schroeder heard the group and was mightily impressed. In an interview with Bill Dahl, Schroeder said, "James

Purify was the lead singer, and Robert Lee Dickey was the guitar player. And Dickey did the blues, soulful harmony parts for James. When I say soulful, he was more of the black soulful part of the act…James was more of the Sam Cooke polished R&B singer." Schroeder signed them, and soon they were off to Muscle Shoals to record some tracks.

But to make recordings, singers must have material, and that was something that Dickey and Purify did not have. Nor did they have a name—at this point, they were simply two individuals with good voices. First Schroeder set about finding a record for Dickey, and he chose a song written by Dan Penn and Spooner Oldham, "I'm Your Puppet." Penn had recorded the song the year before and released it as a single on MGM, but the record went nowhere. Despite the fact that Schroeder felt it would be a good song for Dickey, "I don't think either one of them liked the song, because it wasn't R&B enough to suit [them]," Schroeder told Dahl. "I said, 'Guys, if you'll just work with me on this, I'm telling you, I'm trying to cut a hit record not just for the black market, I'm trying to cut a record that white people will love too'…Dickey just couldn't get it, man. He was trying so hard to sing the lead like I wanted…James Purify said, 'Hey, man, here's what he's talking about.' He started doing the lead. Wow! Then I said, 'Dickey, you do the harmony.'" The sound worked so well, "they agreed to be a duet," though as of yet, they were unnamed.

That recording session has often been called one of the most grueling sessions in music history. Schroeder noted, "It was a twenty-something-hour session, 'cause we were cutting mono. You had to get it all in one time. I mean, it was just incredible. Then you've got [to] come back and do your overdubs." The long session took its toll on Dickey, who in a 2000 interview with the *Florida Democrat* said of "I'm Your Puppet," "I hated it. It was originally intended to be the B-side. But things got changed...I sang it for 23 hours straight (in the studio), that's why I hate it. And the last one, the last take was the one they decided to go with."

But Schroeder knew it was a winner. "I called Larry Utall [at Bell records] and I said, 'Larry...I'm telling you, I just cut a great record.' And he said, 'What's the name of the act?' Well, I knew Robert Dickey—his name was Robert, and Bobby's a nickname for Robert. And Purify...was the funkiest soulful name I ever heard in my life...And I named 'em James and Bobby Purify on the telephone, talking to Larry Utall. And Larry said, 'Wow, what a name!' I said, 'Yeah, it is funky, man, isn't it?'"

"I'm Your Puppet" was released in September 1966, and it eventually peaked at #5 on the R&B charts and #6 on the pop charts. However, a problem arose that would ultimately have far-reaching effects. Despite the fact that the group was successful and was playing big venues, they weren't seeing any of the record's profits. Dickey told the *Democrat*, "We were young, we thought money was coming through our manager but it never was. It was a lesson...I asked (our manager), 'If the record sold 1 million copies, then where's the money?' He didn't have an answer." Schroeder told Dahl it was because "none of the labels shared the profits like they do today," and he was given only "1,500 bucks and eight percent" of sales by Bell for the rights to the record—and Utall balked at that as being too generous. As a result, the artists themselves never saw much of the money, which is unfortunately a pretty common story.

For their second single, they recorded "Wish You Didn't Have to Go," and though it's a beach favorite as well, Schroeder told Dahl, "That was another Penn and Oldham song. It's a nice little record. That wouldn't have been my choice as the follow-up of 'I'm Your Puppet.'" Utall apparently really liked the record though, "and I went along with him. It was a fair record...It's not on my 'Favorite records that I produced' list." The record was a moderate hit, climbing to #38 on the pop charts. For their next release, they covered the Five Du-Tones raucous hit "Shake a Tail Feather," which had hit #51 for that group in 1963. Schroeder says, "I thought I could cut a good record on it, and we did…what a great, fun record. Melba Moore and Ellie Greenwich and I were out there in the studio beating our beer cans on a table…screaming and having fun. I wanted to create a party environment." The record climbed to #25 on the pop charts.

The group's next release didn't break into the Top 40, but their subsequent record, "Let Love Come Between Us," would be their second-biggest hit. Schroeder said someone brought him the song, and he knew it was right for the Purifys, and he specifically chose it because "I was cutting a beach song." The original version had been recorded by an Alabama group called the Rubber Band, whose frontman, John Townsend, would later go on to fame with the Sanford Townsend Band (see the entry for "Smoke from a Distant Fire"). "Let Love Come Between Us" was written by Rubber Band members Johnny Wyker and Joe Sobotka, and a demo the group recorded got them an invitation to CBS Records in New York. "We spent two evenings from midnight to dawn in the studio recording," Townsend told me in an interview for this book. "'Let Love Come Between Us' came out of that session. CBS sent out promo copies to hundreds of radio stations, and within a couple of months, it went to #1 in twenty major cities in the U.S. and Columbia didn't even know it was their record. Therefore no records were in the stores while it was on the air, and we didn't know enough about the business to take things to the next level. It was what was called a turntable hit…Some months later, James and Bobby Purify [did it]. When I heard their version on the radio, we knew it was us that should have had the big record but were proud of it just the same." The Purifys' version went to #23 on the pop charts, and Schroeder said he had achieved his goal of cutting "a real good beach hit. It's one of my favorite records that I cut on the Purifys."

It would be James and Bobby Purify's last Top 40 hit. The group would go on to record some moderately successful songs after that, but the wear and tear of travel and the fact that the group was seeing very little money from their recordings led Dickey to quit by 1972. "I probably could've pressed the [money] issue and gotten what was coming to me," Dickey told the *Democrat*, "but I'm an easygoing person and I don't like to leave enemies behind me, so I left." James Purify eventually brought in Ben Moore to sing as Bobby Purify, and though their re-recording of "I'm Your Puppet" in 1976 went to #12 in the UK, it was their last chart record.

The New Wave

For a group that wasn't around for long and that is perhaps not as well known today as some of their late '60s contemporaries, James and Bobby Purify recorded some incredible music, and today "I'm Your Puppet," "Wish You Didn't Have to Go" and "Let Love Come Between Us" all rank as beach music classics.

Sanford Townsend Band

"Smoke from a Distant Fire"
1977, Billboard #9
Warner 8370

I went over to see Ed [Sanford] one morning, and he had been up all night because he'd been kept awake by his roommate, Steven Stewart, who was a serious musician and who'd stay up late playing classical guitar," Sanford Townsend Band co-founder John Townsend told the author. "Well, Ed was angry, because he hadn't had any sleep, and he told Steven, 'When are you going to knock that crap off and write something that's gonna make you some money?' Steven turned around—he was making coffee and still had his guitar around his neck—and he said, 'Anybody can write that crap!' and he starts playing this great riff he'd made up. Ed and I looked at each other and said, 'Hey, that's pretty cool!' Well, in no time at all, a song that essentially started as a joke became 'Smoke from a Distant Fire'—and wound up making us a great deal of money," Townsend said. That "joke" became a modern beach classic and a Top 10 hit nationwide, as well.

"I was in college at the University of Alabama, and my friends and I were seriously influenced by blues and music like that," Townsend said. "We kept seeing the Swingin' Medallions and John McElrath, and so we decided to start a similar-type group. We had a seven-piece band and called ourselves the Magnificent Seven, and almost overnight we became the most popular band on campus and played all the fraternity parties," Townsend said. Then

The Sanford Townsend Band. *Courtesy of John Townsend.*

the group started to get a little more exposure, eventually becoming a part of the Gulf Coast club scene. "Some of our first gigs were at Dauphin Island and beaches like Pensacola, Destin, places like that. You might say we had 'Sand in Our Shoes' early on!" Eventually, they even played a few times with the Swingin' Medallions, but when "Double Shot" took off, the Medallions started touring and playing bigger venues. "There was a club called Old Hickory where the Medallions had been the house band, and it was a hive of activity every night, especially during the summer. They needed a band because the Medallions were touring, so they hired us. We played there that summer, and that was the beginning of our beach music career." Townsend says there was another group that played at a club down the street, the Rockin' Gibraltars, and Ed Sanford was a member of that band. Townsend, Sanford and a few others then went on to found a band called Heart (no relation to the '80s band of the same name) and moved to California, and then later, he and Sanford went out on their own.

"By that time, Sanford and I had become writing partners and had written maybe a dozen songs together. We were just taking a crack at it, realizing that was where the money was in the business, when you can write and reap the publishing rewards of your own songs. Ed and Steve Stewart were living in a duplex down in Hollywood, and I'd go hang out with them every day. Ed had a little piano, and Steven was a guitar player and one of those people who would actually sit up all night with a music stand in front of him thinking that if he couldn't be Bach, then life wouldn't be worth living," Townsend says.

"I go over one morning, and Ed had been up all night because he'd been kept awake by Steve playing in the next room, so Sanford says, 'When are you going to knock that crap off and write something that's gonna make you some money?'" That's when Stewart came up with the now famous riff as a joking answer to Sanford's challenge, and Sanford and Townsend got on board pretty quickly. "We sat down at the piano and started the song using Steven's riff, and Sanford said, 'I think this will fit a poem I wrote in college—check out these lyrics and see if they work for you.' This poem he'd written when he was at Auburn was actually called 'Smoke from a Distant Fire.' He'd had this girlfriend who was fooling around on him, and I thought it was a great image. I don't remember anything else about the poem—we just took the title from it. The part about 'Don't let the screen door hit you on the way out' we of course borrowed from the idioms in our language!

"We then decided we needed a producer, and we wanted the best, so we got Jerry Wexler. We were the first group he'd produced—he'd always worked with solo artists like Ray Charles and Aretha Franklin. He made Barry Becket co-producer, because he had a great musical mind and he could assess material and get the most out of it. Part of our deal with Barry was that in addition to his percentage on the record, he got $5,000. Barry didn't pocket the money, and he hired a promotion man instead. He got 'Smoke' on twenty-five to thirty stations in Alabama, Mississippi and Georgia, and that was the springboard for us and for the song going national. The next week, one of the Warner Brothers guys walked in and said, 'Hey, this record's just picked up thirty stations in the Southeast in a week. We need to get on this record.' Well, the minute they did, stations in LA and Boston went big on it, and from that point, it was game over. I can remember exactly where I was when I heard 'Smoke' for the first time come out over the radio, and I tell you, it's an experience that's unparalleled. You know you've made it. I had a similar experience in Rome, walking around not far from the Vatican. I was walking by some old courtyard, and I heard the song spiraling down from some apartment through those three-thousand-year-old walls, and I said, 'Okay, we've really made it!' It was kinda cool."

The Sanford Townsend Band. *Courtesy of John Townsend.*

The song went to #9 on the Billboard charts and #1 on Cashbox and was one of the biggest songs of the year. Soon beach music lovers picked up on it because it had just the right beat for shagging, and so it quickly became a mainstay of the shag-club circuit. Townsend says that makes sense, because "most definitely old R&B and beach music influenced the sound of the song. We had started as a band playing Otis Redding, Little Anthony and the Imperials, Sam and Dave, the New Orleans music, the Muscle Shoals stuff, mostly by black artists. It was the music of the day, and when it came time to do our own songs, they came out of the music we were really in love with."

Although they only had the one really big hit, the band toured with Fleetwood Mac, Jimmy Buffett, Foreigner and a number of other top acts. Ed Sanford would later co-write "I Keep Forgettin'" with Michael McDonald, and though Sanford and Townsend have since gone their separate ways, Townsend says he still gets a thrill out of playing "Smoke from a Distant Fire." "I've never stopped playing it, and it always gets a great reaction. I remember when we played in Myrtle Beach, and there was a great crowd. After we played the song, people came up and said, 'You sound just like that guy who sang that song,' and I'd say 'Well, that's

because I *am* that guy!' Other people would say, 'I never knew you guys were white!' For someone with my musical roots, that's one of the greatest compliments I could ever have. When I was playing the Carolinas, I found out what a big beach music record 'Smoke from a Distant Fire' had been, and that's pretty special." As any beach music lover would attest, "Smoke from a Distant Fire" has always been a special song too, and perhaps that's no surprise given it came from two southern boys who grew up listening to and playing music, much of which has now been considered classic beach music for decades.

Shades of Blue

"Oh How Happy"
1966, Billboard #12
Impact 1007

After Motown bought out Impact in late '67, we saw the handwriting on the wall," Shades of Blue frontman Nick Marinelli told the author. "Motown was like any other big corporation, and they'd buy up record companies, take the stable and get rid of the competition. They kept booking us in shows, but they weren't really interested in developing anything new for us or promoting us as a group. But music was changing too, and that's when we decided to hang it up." But before they did, Shades of Blue had one truly monster hit in 1966's "Oh How Happy," a song that would become a shag favorite on jukeboxes throughout the Carolinas.

Shades of Blue was a Detroit-area group that got their start in high school as the Domingos, consisting of Dan Guise, Bob Kerr, Ernie Dernai and Nick Marinelli. The group played mainly local gigs, singing doo-wop and R&B songs and hoping to land a recording contract. Soon after high school, Guise decided to leave the group, but fortunately a replacement was at hand. "We'd been at various clubs at the time while we were out there banging around, and Linda showed some interest in singing," Marinelli said. "She started dating Bobby, and one thing led to another. She was singing in the choir at church, had a good voice, knew music, so it just kind of fell into place."

The Shades of Blue. *Courtesy of Nick Marinelli.*

With new member Linda Allen, the Domingos continued to search for that elusive recording contract. Fortunately, they were friends with some members of the Reflections, who had gone to #6 on the charts with 1964's "Just Like Romeo and Juliet" on the Golden World label. "They lived just a few blocks from us and led us over to Golden World to do a few demos," Marinelli noted. The Reflections recommended them to Golden World owner Ed Wingate, and though he liked their sound, he didn't sign them because he told them he didn't want to sign another white vocal group. Fortunately, their recordings caught the ear of John Rhys, "an independent producer working out of Golden World who'd been a producer in New York and was working at Motown some, and who had also worked with the Newbeats" (of "Bread and Butter" fame). Rhys took an interest in the group, but "he said the name of the group wasn't going to cut it, that it sounded too much like Dominoes. So we all hashed out possible names, and being that we were a blue-eyed soul group, we wanted 'blues' in our name, so we settled on Shades of Blue."

With a new name, they needed a new song, and fate smiled on them again when they crossed paths with a songwriter and performer who would help them get their first big hit. "While we were working doing backup vocals and demos at Golden World, Edwin Starr was there," Marinelli said. "He heard us sing and liked our sound. Well, he had an idea for a song he hadn't finished called 'Oh How Happy.' We all sat down together and finished it, and we even contributed some of the wording and the chorus. But we never got co-writing credit because at the time we were young and stupid and didn't know that we could have and should have."

Despite the fact that they didn't get the writing co-credit, they had the sound down just right, and after they recorded the song in the late fall of 1965, Rhys took the record to Harry Balk at Impact Records, who signed the group to a contract. But the record's release, and success, took the group by surprise. "We had a lot of songs we had recorded already in the can. You never know what the record company is going to release at a certain time, so we kind of went on about our business—we were still in college at the time. We were out one evening with some girls, and 'Oh How Happy' came on the radio on a local station. We're in the car, and we said, 'That's our song!' We were surprised, so we called the record company, who said they had released it and were starting to push on it. Everything just took off." In fact, the record was released in March 1966 and almost immediately shot to #1 in several local markets and would eventually ascend the national charts as well, going to #12 on the pop charts and #7 on the R&B charts. Predictably, the group's fortunes changed overnight. "We wanted to at least finish that year of college, but as soon as we were out of school we hit the road. We were out on the road for about a year; we hardly had a chance to take a breath." The group went on a national tour and appeared on *Where the Action Is* and several other television shows, and so expectations were high for their follow-up single.

That's where things started to go wrong. "We had a battle as to what we wanted to release as our second song, and the biggest problem was that 'Lonely Summer' was released late in August, but it should have been released in June right as 'Oh How Happy' was starting to move back down the charts," Marinelli told me. "I think it was a bad decision to release it so late, but like a lot of groups, we didn't have much input back then." "Lonely Summer," which had also been written by Starr, lacked the cohesive sound of "Oh How Happy" and peaked at #72. Another release, 1966's "Happiness," peaked at #78, but even though these songs didn't do as well as "Oh How Happy," they all charted, and considering that they released an album in September, 1966 had been a very successful year.

But as the group came to learn, success wasn't taking quite the tangible form that it should have. "At Impact, we were the big moneymaker in the company at the time, and of course they started seeing residuals coming in. But we were out on the Dick Clark tour, and we were hearing the other artists talking about the royalty checks they were getting, and we're going, 'Wait a second, we haven't gotten any royalty checks.' Though we were making money on the road, the company was sucking up our royalties and using them to promote other Impact artists like Mitch Ryder and the Detroit Wheels and the Volumes—they were using our income to produce them." That didn't make for a good marriage between the group and the label, and after a couple more singles that weren't well promoted, the group sensed that their careers were at a standstill. When Motown bought up Impact and its catalog and then didn't seem interested in giving them new songs or promoting them, they decided it was time to leave Impact.

"But music was changing too," Marinelli told me. Indeed, by the late '60s, the great harmonizing and vocals that had been a mainstay of the group's repertoire were not as fashionable as they once had been. As a result, they called it quits as performers about 1970. They reunited for a while in the mid-'70s and recorded some new songs that have never been released. "We cut a few things, but the others, their hearts weren't in it," Marinelli said. "It wasn't meant to be." The group broke up again, and the other original members got out of show business while Marinelli did television production work.

Marinelli eventually went back into music, and "I hooked up with a group called the Valadiers. They'd lost their lead singer to the Reflections and were looking for another. They brought me in, and we did a show in Wilmington, Delaware, and I sang 'Oh How Happy.' Five thousand people stood up on their feet. Well, afterwards the guys said, 'You know what, you've obviously got a lot bigger hit than we do. How about if we work with you as the Shades of Blue?' We did, and I worked with them for six years before deciding to go out on my own."

Marinelli is still in the business, "working on a new record and writing some new songs." As for "Oh How Happy," Marinelli says he "really appreciates" that beach music lovers like the record. He knows that he helped create a timeless hit—and beach music lovers know it too.

The Spinners

"TRULY YOURS"
1966, Billboard #111
Motown 1093

"I'LL BE AROUND"
1973, Billboard #3
Atlantic 2904

"ONE OF A KIND (LOVE AFFAIR)"
1973, Billboard #11
Atlantic 2962

"COULD IT BE I'M FALLIN' IN LOVE"
1973, Billboard #4
Atlantic 2927

"WAKE UP SUSAN"
1976, Billboard #56
Atlantic 3341

On 'One of a Kind (Love Affair),' the line near the end simply said, 'I just want to hug her,'" Spinners lead singer Bobbie Smith told the author. "Well, some disc jockey broadcast that the line said, 'I just want to f**k her,' so we had to go back into the studio and clean up that one line. Today you can say anything you want on a record, and it seems like the bigger scandal, the bigger your career gets. But not back then—we had to change it, even though that's not what it said at all." Certainly the 1970s were simpler times, but the music was good enough that it was probably worth putting up with a few censorship issues to produce those songs that became beach music classics. And few groups in the 1970s produced as much good music as the Spinners.

The Spinners. *Courtesy of Bobbie Smith.*

The Spinners got their start in 1954 as the Domingoes and originally consisted of members Billy Henderson, Henry Fambrough, C.P. Spenser, Pervis Jackson and James Edwards. Edwards was soon replaced by Bobbie Smith, and Spencer would leave and be replaced by George Dixon. By 1961, they had renamed themselves after those spinning car hubcaps and had their first real shot at success on Tri-Phi with "That's What Girls Are Made For," which went to #27 on the charts. Other than one more low-charting single, further success eluded them on Tri-Phi, but the label was bought out by Motown and so the group began a new phase of their career. "We went to Motown in 1964," Smith told me, and he noted that though they had some moderate hits there—"I'll Always Love You" went to #35 in 1965, and "Truly Yours" went to #111 in 1966—none of their other releases charted in the 1960s, despite the fact that he felt that they were high-quality songs. "We had some real good stuff at Motown that wasn't getting promoted, songs like 'Truly Yours.' In Detroit, we knew a lot of the DJs, and we'd take our records out ourselves and do the promotion and interviews at the radio stations. They played 'Truly Yours,' and then all of a sudden they weren't playing it anymore. We called and asked why and they said, 'Marvin Gaye has a new song, and we got orders from Motown to take yours off and put his on.' So they'd play Marvin's or whoever else's Motown was pushing and take ours off. I thought we did some great songs at Motown, as good as a lot that was being recorded there, but we seemed to get lost in the shuffle."

Smith says another reason they weren't appreciated at Motown may have been due to his lead vocals. "I always did the leads, but I had a soft smooth voice, and at Motown they seemed to go for a raspier voice, like David Ruffin of the Temptations on 'Ain't Too Proud to Beg' or Levi Stubbs on the Four Tops' 'Bernadette.' My voice was soft and smooth, and I started to feel like I wasn't strong enough as we kept getting overlooked. That's when we brought G.C. Cameron in. He had the ability to sing Motown style." When Cameron joined, he did bring a different sound to the group, and he had some close connections as well. As Cameron told the author, Stevie Wonder was a friend, and one night "he told me, 'I wrote a song for you.' I asked him what it was, and he had me take him to his house and he started playing this song on his electric piano. The song was 'It's a Shame.'"(for the whole story behind "It's a Shame," see *Carolina Beach Music: The Classic Years*). "It's a Shame" raced to #14 on the pop charts and indicated the Spinners' true potential, but the group was ready to leave Motown. "We left Motown because they had a lot of groups of the same caliber as the Spinners," Bobbie Smith said. "They had a staff of writers, and naturally the writers had a choice about who to work with. If you were an artist with a hit, like Marvin Gaye or the Temptations, that's who the producers wanted to work with. When you had a hit you needed to follow a hit with another record, but at Motown, even if we had a hit, it might be another year before we had another record. It was like starting all over. So when our contract was up, we decided to leave. Aretha Franklin was a good friend of ours, and she thought Atlantic would be a good place for us because they didn't have a lot of groups playing the kind of music we were." So the group changed labels, minus Cameron, who stayed at Motown to pursue a solo career.

"When we went to Atlantic, we had already recorded four songs, and one, 'Oh Lord I Wish I Could Sleep,' was about to be released. But at the last minute they called us and said, 'Do you guys want to go with your song, or do you want to do another session?' We asked why, and they said it was because we had a chance to have Thom Bell produce us. They gave Thom a choice to work with anyone there, and he chose us. He said he used to be the piano player at the Uptown Theatre, and he remembered hearing us do 'That's What Girls Are Made For,' and the song stuck in his mind because he liked the harmony. So when he saw our name on the Atlantic roster, he said, 'I'll take them.' It was a great marriage that brought us our great success." So Bell joined the group in Detroit, and they went into the studio and recorded "I'll Be Around," "How Could I Let You Get Away," "Could It Be I'm Fallin in Love" and "Just You and Me Baby." Smith says at the end Bell said, "'Well I'm going back to Philadelphia, and when I come back, you'll be #1.' Of course we'd heard that before! But to make a long story short, three of the songs were million sellers."

They almost misfired on their first effort for Atlantic, however. "'I'll Be Around' was actually the B-side of the first record," Smith said. "'How Could I Let You Get Away' was the A-side, but it was moving up the charts slowly, and I said, 'We've got to turn this record over.' We did, and it shot right to the top." The decision paid off, and while "How Could I Let You Get Away" did go to #77 and #14 on the R&B charts, "I'll Be Around" went to #3 on the pop charts and #1 on the R&B charts. They followed that with Smith singing lead on "Could It Be I'm Falling in Love," which went to #4 on the pop charts but also went to #1 on the R&B charts. Despite having two straight hits, after twenty years in the business, Smith really wasn't convinced they had made it. "I had gotten a job because I was getting to the point where I was thinking, 'It ain't gonna happen' and was thinking about giving up music. In show business, you can't hold a steady job, but you had to have one because you have one of those mediocre hits and you go out of town and work for a while with the band and then you're back to zero. So I always tried to have part-time jobs in between. I had just gotten a good job at the GM building with good benefits, so I had to make the decision after we recorded those songs with Thom. I had to decide if I wanted to keep that job or try one more time. I asked GM for a leave of absence, and they wouldn't give it to me. So I decided to take one last chance, and it was the right one."

It was another good decision, and after "One of a Kind (Love Affair)" was released and went to #11 and became their third straight #1 record on the R&B charts, it was clear the Spinners were going to be around a while. But for the first time, the group was also involved in controversy over a song's lyrics. Philippé Wynne sang lead on the tune, and some listeners thought he sang, "One of a kind love affair/Makes you want to love her/You just got to f**k her, yeah…" Atlantic felt like they needed to make sure that the song was radio-worthy, so they sent the group back into the studio. "What a difference a day makes," Smith says. "Just because some DJ thought that, we had to go back into the studio and clean up that one line. When we were coming up, you did everything you could to protect your career, because one scandal could end it all. So we didn't think anything about being told to do it—we just went in and cleaned it up. If a disc jockey said he thought it said that, we wanted to clear it up for everybody."

The controversial moment over, the group would go on to an unbelievable level of success with songs like "Ghetto Child," "Mighty Love," "Rubberband Man" and their #1 song with Dionne Warwick, "Then Came

You." A song they would release right before "Rubberband Man" in 1976, "Wake Up Susan," has also become very popular on the beach music scene, even though it peaked at #56 on the pop charts. "We used to do 'Wake Up Susan' in our act, and I really liked it," Smith said. "When you put a song out and you want it to be a nationwide hit, and sometimes it is surprising that songs are big in the Carolinas and not other places. But 'Wake Up Susan' was a great song."

The group would go on to record for many years, charting with many more national hits as well as records more appreciated in the Carolinas than elsewhere. Smith notes that 1983's "'City Full of Memories' was big in the Carolinas, though it didn't make any noise anywhere else. It wasn't a national hit, but it was a hit in the Carolinas." But for all the hits on all the levels, Smith believes it's the group's chemistry that led to their success. "We were always the type of group who didn't let success go to our heads—we learned a long time ago that you can't take an ego to the bank. Philippé was the strongest voice and had a lot of charisma on stage, so sometimes he sang lead. You'll hear some smooth ballads that Henry was singing lead on, because that was the type of voice he had. Then you'll hear one I'm lead on, or G.C. when he was with us, and so on. We never looked at any one person as the lead—it was whoever the song fit. We don't care who is singing lead on the song because we're all the Spinners. We don't let those egos get in the way." That team spirit has served them well for over five decades now, making them one of the most successful groups in the annals of beach music, and popular music, history.

The Spiral Starecase

"She's Ready"
1970, Billboard #72
Columbia 45048

A lot of times, we might just be driving around and hear a song that would come on the radio, and somebody would say, 'Maybe we should record that,'" Spiral Starecase lead singer Pat Upton told me. "If we heard a little-known song and thought, 'That's gonna be a hit,' we'd jump on it, and that's what we did there." The song in this case was "She's Ready," a slightly different version of a song the Poppies had first released in 1966. The Spiral Starecase had had a hit with the #12 smash "More Today Than Yesterday" just a year before (see *Carolina Beach Music: The Classic Years*), and the group hoped with "She's Ready" that chart success would come once again; instead, it would be their last single release, as the group fell apart after years of dissension and controversy.

The group started as a Sacramento combo known as the Fydallions, and they soon evolved into a five-piece group consisting of Harvey Kaye, Dick Lopes, Bobby Raymond, Vinnie Parello and lead vocalist Pat Upton. In 1967, they signed with Columbia Records, which changed the name of the group to the "Spiral Starecase," deliberately misspelling it so as to not too closely imitate its source, the movie *The Spiral Staircase*. Their first record, "Baby What I Mean," didn't go anywhere, and Upton said that then "Columbia suggested someone in the group write songs, so I was the one.

I'd had the title 'More Today Than Yesterday' for a couple of years and was jamming with a friend, and he showed me a passing chord that I loved. I knew I would never use that chord with the stuff we were doing and decided the only way was to write a song and use it, and I did. When the chorus came around 'I love you more today than yesterday' just fell right into place." The song raced to #12 on the charts and would eventually sell more than one million copies and earn the group a gold record.

Though the group should have been riding high with their newfound chart success, the reality of the situation was that things were bad—so bad, in fact, that the group members had started to go their separate ways. "We were breaking up and were not together as a band when 'More Today Than Yesterday' came out and became a hit," Upton said. The problem was that the group's manager had been misappropriating funds, people weren't getting paid and it was directly affecting the group's ability to perform. "Once we were flying out to do a performance, and we got to LAX and all of our gear was out on the street because our manager bought our tickets with a stolen credit card," Upton noted. "Another time, we were working at the Flamingo Hotel and we bought a PA system, and then we found out that the money we were giving our manager every week to pay for the PA was not being paid and so they came to repossess it. It was one thing after another. But the incident with the PA system was the final straw, and a couple of members said, 'I'm done,' and we were dead in the water, so to speak."

But then something remarkable happened—"'More Today' started playing on the radio, and everybody jumped back on board," he said. The group toured with Three Dog Night, Creedence Clearwater Revival, Sly and the Family Stone and the Beach Boys and appeared on *American Bandstand*. They cut an album to showcase "More Today Than Yesterday" and released "No One for Me to Turn To" as a single. Because it only charted at #52, the group looked for another big single that would take them back to the heights they had reached with "More Today," and that's where "She's Ready" came into the picture.

The song, written by soon-to-be country music songwriting and producing greats Billy Sherrill (who would later co-write "Stand By Your Man" with Tammy Wynette and write "The Most Beautiful Girl" for Charlie Rich) and Glenn Sutton (who later produced "I Never Promised You a Rose Garden" for then wife Lynn Anderson and wrote "The Beer that Made Milwaukee Famous Made a Loser Out of Me"), had been recorded by girl-group the Poppies as *"He's* Ready" in 1966. The song stalled at #106, and so as a relatively unknown song, it was a good choice

The Spiral Starecase. *Courtesy of Candy Kaye.*

for a cover version by the Spiral Starecase. "We didn't have any say on which recordings were released as singles. Columbia Records and the producer, Sonny Knight, made those decisions," Upton says. Whoever picked it, it was a good choice for a cover, and though the Poppies had released a vocal-heavy version with very little backing instrumentation, the added horns and lush orchestration combined with Upton's always vibrant vocals made the Starecase version a superb track.

Unfortunately, "She's Ready" only reached #72 on the charts, "and it was our last charting single because that's when the group split up for good," Upton said. The problems with management and internal disagreements because of it, coupled with the group's failure to find another follow-up hit, forced the group to finally call it quits in 1970. The guys all went their separate ways, and Upton says he "stayed around LA and did song commercials, sang demos for people and worked in a trio called Old Friends for a few years. I released one single on RCA, and it didn't do anything. It just didn't happen." Kaye put together a new lineup and kept the band's name alive by touring for many years afterward.

Ultimately though, Upton regrets that things went down like they did and believes "the band would have probably stayed together if [the manager] would have taken care of things." Yet despite recording only a few singles, they managed to produce two beach music classics. Not only is the better-known "More Today Than Yesterday" a mainstay of the beach music scene, but "She's Ready" is a fine, shaggable tune as well.

Edwin Starr

"Stop Her On Sight (S.O.S.)"
1966, Billboard #48
Ric Tic109

Edwin Starr wasn't born with that showbiz-friendly name; in fact, he was born Charles Edwin Hatcher. Raised in Cleveland, Ohio, in high school he joined a group called the FutureTones, a successful group that appeared on a local television show, backed up Billie Holiday at a nightclub and even cut a single for Tress Records. However, before the group was able to build any real momentum, Hatcher was drafted in 1960. After returning to civilian life, he joined the Bill Doggett Combo as a singer, and it was there that the group's manager, Don Briggs, suggested that he change his name to "Starr" (with the extra *r*) since Briggs was convinced that he was destined to be a star.

Starr had been doing some songwriting by this point, and based on the popularity of the James Bond movies, he'd written a song called "Agent Double-O-Soul." He told Doggett he wanted to record it, and Doggett, probably reluctant to have his singer go out on his own, downplayed the idea. Starr was persistent, however, and landed an audition at Ed Wingate's Ric Tic Records in Detroit. In 1965, he was able to record his single, just the fourth release for the new label. In order to get the best sound possible, the backup music was provided by the famous Funk Brothers, the studio musicians who, of course, provided the music on the great hit records by the Supremes, Four

Tops, Temptations and other acts at crosstown rival label Motown. The musicians would moonlight from time to time, unbeknownst to label founder Berry Gordy, and so by contributing their pulsing rhythms to Starr's distinctive vocals, they helped the song rise to #8 on the R&B charts and #21 on the pop charts; Starr was on his way.

Starr was on his way in more ways than as just a single artist though. He followed up "Agent" in 1966 by not only charting with his own songs "Back Street" (#95 pop) and "Headline News" (#84), but he also did a vocal accompaniment on the Holidays' "I'll Love You Forever" (#63) and wrote "Lonely Summer" for the Shades of Blue (#72). Most famously, he also wrote "Oh How Happy," Shades of Blue's biggest hit, which went to #12 (see the entry in this book). Then came one of his most brilliant moments, a song he had co-written with Albert Hamilton and Richard Morris, "Stop Her On Sight (S.O.S.)."

Rock critic Dave Marsh compares "Stop Her On Sight" to Starr's other early recordings by noting that of his early releases, "it's this one that's got the goods, one of the greatest non-Motown Motown discs ever cut, with the same booting backbeat, the same thunderous baritone sax riffs, and a vocal as tough and assured as any of the early Marvin Gaye's." Of course, the reason for that Motown sound was the presence, once again, of the Funk Brothers, but they weren't there because Berry Gordy was a team player willing to share his musicians with others in the music industry—in fact, far from it. Gordy had learned after the session for "Agent Double-O-Soul" that the Funk Brothers had moonlighted at Ric Tic and had fined the musicians $100 each. Ric Tic owner Eddie Wingate caught wind of this and, incensed, reportedly showed up at Motown and paid each of them back $200 each. Consequently, the guys were a lot more agreeable about backing up Starr again and did so on "Stop Her On Sight." The combination of Starr's powerful voice and the Motown instrumentation drove the record up to #9 on the R&B charts and #48 on the pop charts. It was so popular in England that it not only went to #11 on the British charts in 1966 but would also chart again in 1968. The song was dynamite.

By this point, Berry Gordy was seeing Ric Tic as a threat, and as Nick Marinelli of Shades of Blue told me in an interview for this book, "Motown [would] buy up record companies, take the stable and get rid of the competition." In 1968, not only did Berry buy Marinelli's label, Impact, but also several other Detroit labels, including Golden World, Maltese, Inferno and perhaps the one he feared the most, Ric Tic. The buyout came as a surprise to Starr; as he noted in a 1994 interview on Palace FM, "I was co-starring at the Apollo Theater with the Temptations and one of the Temptations informed me that I had been signed with Motown. I didn't think that that was possible because no one had told me that Motown bought the company that I was with…I instantly became a Motown artist." Unlike Marinelli, who felt the Shades of Blue were ignored after Motown bought the label, Gordy apparently saw Starr as too valuable a property to let him languish. A number of hits ensued at Motown, such as 1969's "25 Miles," which went to #6 on the R&B and pop charts and, of course, what would become his signature hit, 1970's "War," which went all the way to #1.

By 1973, Starr would move to England and would remain there for the rest of his life. In 2003, at the age of sixty-one, he died of a heart attack, having left a legacy of many great songs that were loved the world over. In the Carolinas, however, it was the Motown-sound-driven "Stop Her On Sight" that has endeared him to beach music lovers for generations.

The Tams

"Hey Girl, Don't Bother Me"
1964/1971, Billboard #41/reissue did not chart
ABC Paramount 10573/ABC Dunhill 4290

"Too Much Foolin Around"
1970, did not chart
1-2-3 1726

"The Tams Medley"
1971, did not chart
Capitol 3050

W e had all wanted to do a medley of our songs, so we talked to Bill Lowery and he had the writers put together 'The Tams Medley'— and we loved it," Charles Pope said. The song would go on to be one of their most popular numbers, a link between the classic Tams beach music of old and the new direction that beach music was heading in during the 1970s. Though the song came out when conflicts with management could have derailed a less established group, the Tams persevered and, in the 1970s, would enjoy one of the most successful runs in their history.

The Tams originally consisted of brothers Joe and Charles Pope, Floyd Ashton (soon to be replaced by Albert Cottle), Robert Lee Smith and Horace Key, and the group took their name from their trademark tam-o'-

The Tams. *Courtesy of Diane Pope.*

shanter hats, which was about all they could afford in the way of costumes. Working with Atlanta song publisher and entrepreneur Bill Lowery, in 1962 the group recorded "Untie Me" for Arlen Records, which climbed to #62 on the Hot 100 and #12 on the R&B charts. ABC-Paramount picked up their contract and gave their music an even broader national release, and their first ABC recording, "What Kind of Fool (Do You Think I Am?)," written by a young songwriter named Ray Whitley, did very well, going to #9 on the Billboard charts. Charles Pope says that he "was surprised by 'What Kind of Fool,'" because he wasn't wild about it and "didn't even want that song to be our second release," but the combination of Whitley's songwriting and the Tams' great voices were a recipe for success. The Tams were clearly on their way.

This led to a long series of national and regional hits, including "Hey Girl, Don't Bother Me," which went to #41, and "Silly Little Girl," which went to #87. Charles Pope recalls that "Silly Little Girl" "was Joe's favorite song. He especially liked to perform it live and would ad-lib a lot of lines that weren't in the song originally. He'd add 'I'll even beg you girl' and things like that." In 1965, they released "I've Been Hurt" ("a favorite with the college kids," Pope said) and, in 1968, "Be Young, Be Foolish, Be Happy," which to many beach music lovers epitomizes the beach music experience. While "Be Young" would only hit #61 on the pop charts, it would sell more than one million copies and be a RIAA-certified gold record. So while the Tams' records weren't always charting high on the pop charts, the group was developing a huge following. (See the complete story behind the early Tams hits in *Carolina Beach Music: The Classic Years.*)

As the 1970s began, the Tams were still going strong, and the group next released another song by Whitley, "Too Much Foolin Around," which Pope says they "recorded in Mississippi on Bill Lowery's own 1-2-3 Label." Though the song didn't make the pop charts, it was another big regional beach music hit. But things were not going well in terms of the relationship between the group and Lowery. Pope says though the group was selling lots of records, very little money was trickling down to the members of the group, and that was causing unrest. The group honored their contract with Lowery nevertheless, and they next released "The Tams Medley" in 1971, a compilation of Whitley-penned hits by the group, including "Hey Girl, Don't Bother Me," "What Kind of Fool (Do You Think I Am)," "You Lied to Your Daddy," "I've Been Hurt," "Laugh It Off" and "Be Young, Be Foolish, Be Happy." Though it failed to chart nationally, it became yet another popular regional hit.

At about this same time, they would have their biggest chart hit—but not in the United States. Due to the Northern Soul boom in England, 1964's "Hey Girl, Don't Bother Me" had found a whole new audience, and upon its re-release in England it went all the way to #1, stayed there for three weeks and was song of the year in the United Kingdom. Pope noted that this was a pleasant surprise, and a highlight of the song's popularity was that "we went over and performed at Top of the Pops with Rod Stewart in 1971." Hoping to capitalize on this success in the States as well, ABC Dunhill re-released the song in the United States in 1971 in a sleeve that said "It's Number ONE in England and the Biggest Selling Record in the U.K. this Year." The song didn't re-connect with audiences here as it had in England, and the United States re-release failed to chart.

Yet despite their continued success into the early 1970s, their relationship with Lowery had reached an all-time low. "Lowery just seemed to get all of the money—he always did," Pope said. "I have paperwork about all kinds of money we were supposed to get for record sales, but we never saw it." Feeling that enough was enough, they finally split with Lowery as their manager, but even then they couldn't make a clean break. "We left Bill sometime in 1972, and even though he stopped managing us, he still did some of our bookings. He and Cotton Carrier had an agency and booked all of our acts. Everyone called them to book the Tams, so he still had control of the booking money." Eventually, the group "went with Harold Thomas from Charleston, and he was the one that put out 'This Precious Moment'" in 1978. Recorded in 1978 in Muscle Shoals, Alabama, "This Precious Moment" was a lushly orchestrated number with a late '70s disco-type dance beat (the flip was a reworking of "Hey Girl, Don't Bother Me" in a late '70s danceable format). Though the song didn't make the Billboard charts, it was a regional favorite, as had been all of their songs.

As the group performed into the 1980s, they would find more great chart success in England, with both "There Ain't Nothing Like Shaggin'" going to #21 on the British charts in 1987 and "My Baby Sure Can Shag" going to #91 in 1988. "What Kind of Fool" was one of the songs featured in the 1989 film *Shag*, and it reintroduced their music to new audiences everywhere. And while the Tams continued to be successful, their old friend and songwriter Ray Whitley was not so lucky. "Ray still comes to see us sometimes, but he's broke and lives in a homeless shelter in Gainesville, Georgia," Pope said. "That's really sad, because he wrote a lot of hits but didn't get his writing royalties."

Today, despite the death of Joe Pope, the Tams continue to "work one hundred days a year after all these years," Charles Pope said. "My son Little Redd started with me and my brother Joe when he was seven years old, and he'll be taking over the Tams. That's why I say the Tams will never die."

Tower of Power

"This Time It's Real"
1973, Billboard #65
Warner 7733

"You Ought to Be Havin' Fun"
1976, Billboard #68
Columbia 3-10409

I had a friend named Jay Spell, a keyboard player, and in fact he played on 'This Time It's Real,'" Tower of Power founder Emilio Castillo told me. "Years after we cut 'This Time It's Real,' he wound up living down in Myrtle Beach, and one day he called me and tried to tell me about beach music. He said, 'You guys have some big songs on the beach music scene.' Well, it didn't make sense to me, because like a lot of people out here [in California], I thought beach music meant Jan and Dean and the Beach Boys. He said, 'Nah, nah, beach music is soul music, R&B, and it's very big here.' So yeah, I know what it is and am *very* aware of it now." And despite the fact that Tower of Power rarely plays in the Southeast these days, nevertheless, "when we get a gig there, the fans flock to see us."

Castillo's entrance into the world of music came as the result of a very big mistake he made as a kid. "My brother, a friend and I were going to the pool one day to scope chicks, you know, and back then, these pastel-colored, muscleman-type T-shirts were really popular," he said. "Well, we went to a store, put two or three of these shirts on under these baggy shirts we had for the pool and decided we'd walk out and steal the shirts." The boys got caught, but it was a life-changing event for them all in many ways. "I had a really short criminal career—it lasted one day because we got caught first time out! After my dad picked us up and we apologized to the store manager and all of that, he got us home and said, 'You and your brother need to think of something that's gonna keep you occupied and off the streets and out of trouble, and if you don't come up with something you can just stay in your room the rest of your lives.' Well, the Beatles had just hit America, and a friend of ours had bought a guitar, and so we said, 'We want to play music.' Dad was the bar manager at the Cabana motel, and they always had show bands. He had taken us there a few times, and I'd noticed that the guy who always seemed to get all the attention was the guy who played the sax. So when he took us to the store and told us we could have any instrument we wanted, I pointed to the sax. We started the band that day, and I've had a band ever since. But it's not like we practiced for years and joined a band; we started the band, *then* learned to play the instruments."

The Tower of Power. *Courtesy of Emilio Castillo.*

Their father's investment in his children's future would pay off well for Castillo—as well as millions of music fans. Even when they started out, "we always sort of leaned towards more soulful stuff. My parents always had real soulful music playing like Dinah Washington, Nat King Cole and Bill Doggett, so I was all about soul music. I patterned myself and my band after those artists, and in fact we called our band the Motowns." Soon Castillo added Doc Kupka to the band, and while Kupka appreciated the band's sound, he believed they could do more than cover tunes. "He said, 'What you're doing with these soul tunes is amazing, and I like how you make them your own. But you need to write your own songs.' I don't think that ever would have occurred to me, but I thought we could give it a try, and the first song we wrote was 'You're Still a Young Man.' We had an audition at the Fillmore, where everyone was trying to get signed by Bill Graham, who had two labels, and he decided to sign us, and that's where it all started."

"You're Still a Young Man" would go to #29 on the charts in 1972, and in 1973, they'd release their biggest hit, "So Very Hard to Go" (#17). Lenny Williams was by then lead vocalist for the group, and his contributions made not only "So Very Hard to Go" a big hit but also the album it was taken from, *Tower of Power*, which went to #15 on the album charts and earned a gold record. The album's sales were also helped by another chart record, the now-classic "This Time It's Real."

"David Bartlett was the main guy who wrote the song. He was a drummer and joined the band later. David had an amazing aptitude for writing, but when he brought it to us, he had less than half of the tune written. He had the chorus, the chords and the first verse. He brought it to us, and we sat down and wrote that tune quick. We added the modulation—the way it goes [singing]—'And I know, I can feel it, this time it's real. And I know, I can feel it…' You know the way it goes up, and it goes down, and it goes up? And so we finished it and were really happy with it," Castillo said. While the single only charted at #65 on the Hot 100, it did hit #27 on the R&B charts, and like many other beach music classics, it found an audience in the Southeast despite its failure to climb high on the national charts.

Several more big albums and hit singles would follow, and in 1976, the group would record another song that many beach music lovers have since adopted as a party-time anthem, "You Ought to Be Havin' Fun." "It was mainly written by Hubert Tubbs, who had replaced Lenny Williams in the group. He came to us, started clapping his hands and singing, 'You ought to be havin' fun,' but that was really about all he had other than the line 'Put your troubles on the run' and the chant, 'You ought to be, you ought to be! You ought to be, you ought to be!' So I wrote the tune, was really excited about it, gave it to the band. The intro, that bass line, was directly inspired by the bass line intro on 'Bad Luck' by Harold Melvin and the Blue Notes. I mean, we didn't steal their line, we made up our own, but it was the inspiration." Like "This Time It's Real," "You Ought to Be Havin' Fun" didn't chart very high either, going only to #68 and #62 on the R&B charts. "That song was one of my heartbreaks," Castillo says. "As a record producer, I felt like I missed the mark on that song. I'm usually good at getting to that place. I have the picture, and I get it there. But in that case, I felt like it fell short. It was good, but not the way I pictured. Then later in my career, I did something that I never do—I redid the song, but it still missed the mark. I'd love to see another artist do that song. I just had a higher ideal for that tune."

"You Ought to Be Havin' Fun" would be the group's last chart single, but today they still play and tour to packed houses everywhere. "We play mostly the Northeast, but the Southeast hasn't been a big market for us for years. We can't seem to get arrested down there! It's not that we don't have fans down there because when we get a gig down there, we see a lot of fans." That's easy to understand, and though the California-based band may play more frequently in the Northeast, no one can argue that the music they make is considered as good as any of the original 1970s tunes that have been adopted as beach music since.

Wild Cherry

"1-2-3 KIND OF LOVE"
1978, did not chart
Epic 6497

The idea for '1-2-3 Kind of Love' came from thinking that it's like seeing someone attractive you have an eye for," Wild Cherry founder and lead singer Rob Parissi told the author. "First, the attraction, second, you imagine and fantasize about them, then, when you get to know them and the two of you fall in love with each other, you think about it being a lasting thing," he said. Parissi, who not only sang lead but also wrote the song, says that's really all there was to it. "I was just thinking 'Motown' when I wrote it. Nothing more, nothing less." Nevertheless, his 1978 composition found an audience on the Carolina beach music scene, even as his band was disintegrating around him.

Wild Cherry got their start in Ohio in 1970, when lead singer Rob Parissi put together a band to play R&B and popular music. They apparently coined their name when Parissi jokingly told the band that maybe they should call themselves Wild Cherry after a box of cough drops he had on hand during an illness. The band liked it, though Parissi himself was less than wild about it. "I just gotten out of the hospital with a week to go to rehearse for our first gig," he told me. "I had had tubes stuck down my throat and still had a sore throat. In the middle of rehearsal one day, the guys said, 'What are we going to call ourselves?' I picked up the cough drops I had on our keyboard player's B-3 and said, 'You can call it Wild Cherry if you want; the band's going to make the name famous if it's good.' They stopped dead and said, 'That's a great name!' I said, 'No, there's no way we're going to name this band Wild Cherry.'

"Well, they fought with me every day until I gave in and said we could call ourselves that for the first gig, but after that, we needed to look for a name. At that first gig, they brought up twenty-five girls at a time that told me what a great name we chose for the band. The guys in the band just wouldn't let me change it. Every time I tried to change it, they'd just bring up more people to disagree at the gigs." So the name stuck, and the band played throughout the Ohio, Pennsylvania and West Virginia corridor. Soon they landed a recording contract and cut several singles in the early '70s before disbanding. Parissi then became the manager of some Bonanza steakhouses, but the lure of music was too strong. Before long he re-formed the band as a quartet, now consisting of himself and Bryan Bassett, Rob Beitle and Allen Wentz. The band had a great local following in the Pittsburgh area, and though they were a rock band, with the emergence of disco, audiences were calling more and more for dance music. As the now legendary story goes, at the 2001 disco in Pittsburgh, black fans kept asking them, "Are you going to play some funky music, white boys?" In between shows one night, Beitle made the comment that they had to "play that funky music, white boy," and a suddenly inspired Parissi immediately wrote out the song on a bar order pad. Soon they recorded the song, Epic picked it up and released it and the rest, as they say, is history. In 1976, the song went to #1 on the pop and R&B charts, the album went platinum and some of the music industry's highest awards followed.

But even in the midst of their success, the band was struggling to find an identity and to simply get along, Parissi says. "The members of the band hated everything, even 'Play That Funky Music,' and getting them to do anything at all was a day-to-day challenge, as they constantly complained about everything that I wrote but never contributed anything progressive regarding material they thought was better or what they thought was 'cool' enough for them…It was like dragging three people you need to cut a track toward getting on the gravy train, constantly. I had to push everything out of all of them."

Despite Parissi's pushing and his skill as writer, after "Play That Funky Music," subsequent singles didn't come close to reaching the success of their #1 record. The year 1977 saw the group release three singles that charted, "Baby Don't You Know" (#43), "Hot to Trot" (#95) and "Hold On" (#61),

Wild Cherry. *Courtesy of Rob Parissi.*

and then in 1978, they released "1-2-3 Kind of Love"—which, oddly enough, despite its longevity on the beach music scene, didn't chart at all. But things had reached a boiling point within the group by then, and there was a total lack of cohesion. "Actually, I'm amazed we got all the way through the '1-2-3' of that tune. It might have only got as far as being a 1 or 2 Kind of Love if they had their way back then," Parissi said. But he does feel the song does a good job of delivering its message about the nature of relationships "in three and a half minutes or so." You "tell a story in three verses, and have one good chorus and a bridge within three and a half minutes, fade it out and call it a good day." Yet even though they were still recording some quality tracks such as "1-2-3," Parissi was fed up with having to fight to motivate the band, and they finally disbanded. "I wish I had a rosier picture to paint for you," he told me, "but the whole Wild Cherry debacle is not a warm and fuzzy memory for me, and I'm quite glad it's a done deal that I don't need to revisit or live over again. But it's all water under the bridge at this point, and I'm grateful for anything good and sustainable that accidentally happened along the way."

Parissi does appreciate, however, that one especially good thing *did* happen along the way as far as beach music lovers are concerned, and that is that

he created a song people like in the Carolinas. "I haven't performed that song live since 1978, but as far as how I feel about how '1-2-3 Kind of Love' ranks among all the songs I wrote, it's not about me after I write and record whatever tune, it's about how people like it and what they think. Obviously, people in 'beach music country' like that song, and for that I'm grateful."

Robert Winters and Fall

"L-O-V-E"
1982, did not chart
Casablanca Album Cut

It was a song that was an afterthought, a cover tune that not only did not chart but also an album cut that was never released as a single. The song's languid journey to beach music fame paralleled that of its singer to chart success; it took him a decade and a half to get a national recording contract, and even then he never once broke the top 100 on the pop charts. Yet against all odds, Robert Winters and Fall's "L-O-V-E" gained recognition in beach music circles and is today regarded as one of the most pleasing and danceable of the early '80s "new" beach music classics.

Detroit-born Robert Winters was stricken with polio as a child, but despite the fact that he was confined to a wheelchair for life, his love of music kept him from lamenting his handicap and the limitations it imposed on him physically. Lovingly nicknamed "Budda" [*sic*] by his friends for his tendency to sit cross-legged in order to rest comfortably, he nurtured his love for music by singing gospel and by teaching himself to play the piano. By the mid-'60s, he had met Ron Murphy, and Murphy noted that though they started recording in 1966, "we didn't release anything until 1968." "Soul Motivation" was in fact released twice on Ron's record label, though neither effort charted. Murphy noted that although "the songs were the quality that Robert wrote in the '80s" and

Decca showed a slight interest in his music, Winters was not able to land a national recording contract.

Winters apparently decided that he had a greater chance at success in California and headed for the West Coast. He performed with a Hispanic/African American group called Spic and Spade, which eventually bowed to pressure and renamed their group Highway Robbery. Winters also made a living doing backup vocals, recording children's songs and doing session work playing the piano as well. Along with Walter Fall Turner and Tony Saunders, they decided to form a new group, settling on the name Robert Winters and Fall as a play on words referencing not only Winters's seasonal-sounding last name but also Turner's middle name. Working with songwriter and producer Jimmy George, who had worked with Smokey Robinson, the Commodores, the Temptations and others, the group recorded "Magic Man," which came to the attention of Clive Davis, leading to the group signing a national recording contract in 1980. *Magic Man* was released on Buddah Records, and the first single, "Magic Man," would "bubble under" the pop charts at #101, the highest a Winters record would ever reach on the pop charts. It did well on the R&B charts, however, going to #11, and garnered the group an appearance on *Soul Train*. In a move that seems especially insensitive today, the record company made Winters stay behind his piano during the show so television audiences could not see that he was handicapped.

The label released two more singles from the album, though only "When Will My Love Be Right" charted (#46, R&B charts). The group then moved to Casablanca, a label that Neil Bogart, formerly head of Buddah, was now running. In 1982, the group released the album *L.O.V.E.*, and though it was mainly filled with ballads, by far the best track is the beach music classic "L-O-V-E." The song is a cover of an Al Green song that peaked at #1 on the R&B charts and #13 on the pop charts in 1975. However, while Green's version has the slow, almost mournful sound for which Green is so well known, Winters's version is bouncy, an energetic song buoyed by Winters's strong, vibrant voice. Why there was no move to release that track as a single is a mystery, especially since one of the album's single releases was a weak cover of the Captain and Tennille's "Do That to Me One More Time" that did not chart. It was the only album Winters would do with Casablanca and his last album or national release of any kind.

Winters's health started to decline rapidly in the 1980s, and he passed away due to complications from an enlarged heart in 1989. While his moment of fame was very brief, and perhaps by some standards not all that famous, he left beach music audiences with one very special tune in "L-O-V-E," beat-for-beat one of the best shag tunes of the early 1980s.

Works Cited

Barker, John. "Summertime's Calling Me." E-mail to the author. September 26, 2011.

Bell, Archie. Telephone interview with the author. September 27, 2012.

Bell, William. Telephone interview with the author. October 11, 2011.

Bogdanov, Vladimir, et. al. *All Music Guide to Soul: The Definitive Guide to R&B and Soul*. San Francisco: Backbeat Books, 2003.

"Box in the Garage—Shades of Blue." MOG. http://mog.com/DashboardDJ856/blog/2844246

Bradford, Bill. Telephone interview with the author. February 17, 2012.

Brown, Clyde. Telephone interview with the author. July 25, 2011.

Butler, Jerry. Telephone interview with the author. October 1, 2012.

Cason, Buzz. *The Adventures of Buzz Cason: Living the Rock n' Roll Dream*. Milwaukee, WI: Hal Leonard Corp., 2004.

Castillo, Emilio. Telephone interview with the author. August 7, 2011.

Curry, Clifford. Telephone interview with the author. October 31, 2011.

Dahl, Bill. "Papa Don Schroeder Reminisces about Producing James and Bobby Purify…" Sundazed.com. http://www.sundazed.com/scene/exclusives/papa_don_exclusive.html. March 18, 2012.

Dawson, Jim, and Steve Propes. *45 RPM: The History, Heroes, and Villains of the Pop Music Revolution.* San Francisco: Backbeat Books, 2003.

Detroit Record Labels. http://www.seabear.se/detroit2.htm.

Drew, Patti. Interview with Bob Abrahamian. www.sittinginthepark.com/index.html.

Elston, Harry. Telephone interview with the author. May 21, 2012.

Gilstrap, Jim. Telephone interview with the author. September 27, 2011.

Goins, Kevin. "Remembering the Esquires." http://www.examiner.com/r-b-music-in-milwaukee/remembering-the-esquires-how-they-got-on-up-from-milwaukee-to-the-music-charts. March 24, 2012.

Gore, Jackie. Telephone interview with the author. July 17, 2011.

Hamilton, Andrew. "Roy Hammond." All-Music. http://www.allmusic.com/artist/roy-hammond-p338312/biography.

Hammond, Roy C. Telephone interview with the author. March 22, 2012.

Haynes, Greg. *The Heeey Baby Days of Beach Music.* N.p., 2005.

Hook, John. *Shagging in the Carolinas.* Charleston, SC: Arcadia, 2005.

Houston, Keith. Telephone interview with the author. August 18, 2011.

James, Gary. Interview with Nick Marinelli of Shades of Blue. http://www.classicbands.com/ShadesOfBlueInterview.html.

Jancik, Wayne. *The Billboard Book of One-Hit Wonders*. New York: Billboard Books, 1990.

Kaye, Candy. "The Spiral Starecase." E-mail to author. April 14, 2010.

Kelly, Red. "James and Bobby Purify: So Many Reasons." The B Side. http://redkelly.blogspot.com/2007/10/james-bobby-purify-so-many-reasons-bell.html.

Knight, Robert. Telephone interview with the author. July 6, 2012.

Lewis, Pete. "Errol Brown: A Fondent Farewell." *B&S Online*. http://www.bluesandsoul.com/feature/377/errol_brown_a_fondent_farewell/. May 17, 2012.

Marinelli, Nick. Telephone interview with the author. February 1, 2012.

Marsh, Dave. *The Heart Of Rock & Soul: The 1001 Greatest Singles Ever Made*. New York: Da Capo Press, 1999.

"Millie Jackson Is Amazing!" http://fourfour.typepad.com/fourfour/2012/02/millie-jackson-is-amazing.html. May 24, 2012.

Parissi, Rob. "Wild Cherry." E-mails to the author. August 8, 9 and 10, 2011.

Parker, Steve. "The Northern Soul Top 500." Steve Parker Micro Site. http://www.rocklistmusic.co.uk/steveparker/northern_soul_top_500.htm.

Pope, Charles. E-mails to the author. June 25, July 11, 23, 25 and 27 and August 28, 2010.

Proctor, Jay. Telephone interview with the author. July 20, 2012.

Reid, Jeff. Telephone interview with the author. March 8, 2012.

Rizik, Chris. "The Friends of Distinction." Soul Tracks. http://www.soultracks.com/friends_of_distinction.htm. May 15, 2012.

Roberts, Kev. *The Northern Soul Top 500*. London: Bee Cool Publishing, 2003.

Scott, Billy. E-mails to the author. November 10, 2010; January 30, 2011; July 6, 2011; March 3, 7, 8, 9, 10 and 11, 2012; September 14, 17, 19, 26 and 27, 2012; and October 1, 2 and 3, 2012.

————. Telephone interview with the author. November 1, 2010; July 7, 2011.

"Shades of Blue History." SOB Entertainment. http://www.sobentertainment.com/history2.html.

Smith, Bobbie. Telephone interview with the author. September 10, 2011.

Smith, John. "Edwin Starr's Early Years." http://www.edwinstarr.info/earlybiog.htm.

"Soulful Kinda Music." http://www.soulfulkindamusic.net/discographies.htm.

"Spiral Starecase." Mclane & Wong Entertainment Law. http://www.benmclane.com/spiral.htm.

Threatt, Sonny. "Sunny and Phyllis." E-mails to author. May 27, 28, 29 and 30 and August 16, 2010.

Tomlinson, Bobby. Telephone interview with the author. August 1, 2010.

Townsend, John. Telephone interview with the author. August 16, 2011.

Trexler, Donny. Telephone interview with the author. March 9, 2012.

Upton, Pat. "More Today." E-mails to author. June 10 and October 19, 2010.

————. Telephone interview with the author. July 7, 2011.

Warner, Jay. *American Singing Groups*. Milwaukee, WI: Hal Leonard Press, 2006.

Washburn, Mark Lawrence Toppmann, and April Baker. "Beach Music Icon General Johnson Dies." *Charlotte Observer*, October 15, 2010. www. charlotteobserver.com/2010/10/15/1761650/beach-music-icon-general-johnson.html.

Weiss, Ed. Telephone interview with the author. August 12, 2010.

Whitburn, Joel. *Billboard Hot 100 Charts—The Sixties*. Milwaukee, WI: Hal Leonard Corp., 1995.

———. *Bubbling Under the Hot 100, 1959–1985*. Menomonee Falls, WI: Record Research, 1992.

———. *Top Pop Singles, 1955–1986*. Menomonee Falls, WI: Record Research, 1987.

———. *Top R&B Singles, 1942–1995*. Milwaukee, WI: Hal Leonard Corp., 1996.

About the Author

D r. Rick Simmons was born and raised in South Carolina, and during the course of his education, he attended Clemson University, Coastal Carolina University and the University of South Carolina, where he completed his PhD in 1997. He currently lives in Louisiana with his wife, Sue, and his children, Courtenay and Cord, though he still spends a portion of the summer at his family home in Pawleys Island, South Carolina. He is the holder of the George K. Anding Endowed Professorship at Louisiana Tech University, where he is currently the director of the Honors Program and the Center for Academic and Professional Development. This is his fifth book, and three of his previous books, *Carolina Beach Music: The Classic Years* (2011), *Hidden History of the Grand Strand* (2010) and *Defending South Carolina's Coast: The Civil War from Georgetown to Little River* (2009), were also published by The History Press.

Visit the Facebook page for
Carolina Beach Music from the '60s to '80s: The New Wave

http://www.facebook.com/
CarolinaBeachMusicFromThe60sToThe80sTheNewWave

DON'T MISS

Carolina Beach Music: The Classic Years

978.1.60949.214.4 * 6 x 9 * 208 PP * 40 IMAGES * $19.99

Just as the dances of beach music have their twists and turns, so, too, do the stories behind the hits made popular in shag haunts from Atlantic Beach to Ocean Drive and the Myrtle Beach Pavilion. In *Carolina Beach Music*, local author and beach music enthusiast Rick Simmons draws on firsthand accounts from the legendary performers and people behind the music. Simmons reveals the true meaning behind "Oogum Boogum," uncovers just what sparked a fistfight between Ernie K. Doe and Benny Spellman at the recording session of "Te-Ta-Te-Ta-Ta" and examines hundreds of other true events that shaped the sounds of beach music.

Visit us at
www.historypress.net